The Essential Guide
to a
Life of Travel

The ABC's of
International Travel

Diann Schindler, Ph.D.

Diann Schindler, Ph.D.

ENDORSEMENTS

"...the writing is vibrant, the content interesting and the reader is immediately drawn in..."The Guide" is very original...combining great advice and information, with very individual experiences and great stories."
-Ann and John Sharples, British World Travelers Living in Spain

"Where was this book when I was on my solo adventure in Greece? I could have saved so much time, money, energy, and worry. "The Essential Guide to a Life of Travel" is the consummate reference guide book: well organized and user friendly! Dr. Schindler's inspirational and moving vignettes take this reference book to a whole new level."
-Constance Vlahoulis, Artist and Curator

"Much like Diann, I caught the travel bug at a very young age. Luckily I've enjoyed traveling extensively for work and play. The downside of my travel has always been the time and effort it takes to plan my trips and the many decisions I have to make while traveling. Imagine how happy I am to have found "The Essential Guide to a Life of Travel." It is a practical, well organized guide that provides just the type of information I need to take my mind off of travel challenges so that I can concentrate on the pleasures ahead. I recommend it for anyone who is getting ready to pack their bags and explore the world."
-Jean Blosser, Ed.D, ASHA Fellow and President,
Creative Strategies for Special Education

"Traveling abroad is beneficial for so many reasons, but most importantly it increases your mental wellbeing and not just in the short term. Traveling opens up so much confidence, happiness and global awareness for your own personal growth. 'The Essential Guide to a Life of Travel,' by Diann Schindler is the perfect resource for anyone thinking of traveling or who travels a lot. There's useful information here to assist you in virtually anything you would need to know to travel abroad! Now go out and do it!"
-Marilyn Ball, Host of the iHeart Radio show Speaking of Travel

DEDICATION

I dedicate this book to my father, SPENCE LEDFORD. He would have been 102 old at the time of this writing. Although he chose to pass up a four-year scholarship at Northwestern University (IL), he, by his own volition, was a scholar, a voracious reader of history, and a lifelong learner.

My father was also a strict conservative. For example, reading paperback books was forbidden and he was dead set against girls going to college. Yet, he had high expectations. He demanded my sister and I learn to work with our hands and obey our husbands.
I exceled in the former and failed in the latter.

Dad always told me I could do anything I wanted to do. That consistent message instilled a level of confidence in me that has remained at my core throughout my life.

I miss him.

Introduction

When I was in elementary school, in the third grade, I remember studying Chile. I was completely drawn to this land of extreme terrain and colorful culture. I wanted to dance and sing like they danced and sang. I imagined how the Andes looked when I could actually see the mountains first hand. I could only dream what *asado, empanada,* and *crudos* tasted like. I longed to eat those foods. And, I especially wanted to meet those smiling children pictured in the Encyclopedia Britannica.

Chile was a world away and I wanted to go!

I remember this third-grade Chile lesson like it was yesterday. I was nine years old and it was the beginning of my relationship with my very own travel bug. It was an insidious, but subtle, gadfly-like bug that gently nagged me long after Mrs. Wilson's geography class.

It latched on and remained secure despite my choice to decline, albeit reluctantly, an opportunity to work overseas for the Federal Bureau of Investigation right after high school. And, although I managed a nine-day tour of Europe, three weeks in Japan, a long week end in Bermuda, and holidays in Mexico, my travel bug became a deep-seated disease. Leaving the subtle approach behind, it reminded me that my desire, now my need, could never be satiated with an occasional jaunt here and there over a twenty-five year career in higher education.

Ah, but the Universe! It always spoke to me; but, of course, I didn't always listen, of course. In the last few years, either it has become louder or I have finally opened up to hear it!

In October of 2015, I went with tennis friends, Ruth Ann and Leon, to Istanbul and Cappadocia. This trip to Turkey became the ultimate tipping point. No longer in denial, I surrendered. Alas, I was free from myself. I embraced my lifelong disease. As a result, my tenacious travel bug was transformed into a sweet, enthusiastic companion that released my free spirit and passion for adventure.

Within three months after the Turkey metamorphosis, I sold my house, my car, and all my worldly possessions, save my guitar, tennis racket and a few pieces of clothing that fit nicely in a medium-sized suitcase. On January 15, 2016, I began my lifelong dream of traveling the world.

At the time of this writing, I had traveled to over thirty countries. I hiked the volcanic mountains of Madeira Island, Portugal; traversed the cliffs of Costa da Morta (aka "Death Coast") in northwestern Spain; climbed the Grand Atlas mountains of Morocco; cruised the Danube River in Austria; sang and played my guitar in Spain, Italy, and Kosovo; attended the French Open Tennis Tournament in Paris and the Italian Open Tennis Tournament in Rome; road a camel in Cappadocia, Turkey; attended opera performances in Italy and Austria; walked the sacred grounds of Auschwitz in Poland; rode horseback to the top of Cusco, Peru; and experienced spiritual surrender to Machu Picchu; and much more.

But, wait! Yes, I did all that! But, what is it about travel that has captured my everything? Yes, it is a clear that the sights and sounds are incredible; knowledge of histories is enlightening and humbling. But, there is more, much more.

The answer is: it is the people.

There is a Moorish proverb: "He who does not travel does not know the value of men." It is easy to think we know how other people live and how other countries look, based on our third grade geography classes, news broadcasts, and socialized stereotypes. But, it is not until we tighten our own shoe laces and step forward to see the world, that we replace myth with fact.

When we experience a stranger's hospitality, meet their families, eat their food, and observe how they treat others and their land, we can start to assign authentic worth to other populations— and to mankind.

For me, travel is incredibly transformative because of the warm and loving individuals I have met from a variety of countries and cultures, and in all walks of life. These acquaintances and extraordinary relationships are ground in mutual respect and curiosities about people and their home countries from all over world.

The passion and commitment people have for their countries and their countrymen have broadened my perspectives. I question myself daily: "Why didn't you do more for your country?"

It is all very humbling. I'm grateful for this growth opportunity and know I have much more to learn.

I invite you to join me, along with the thousands of travelers, and experience, for yourself, the transformational nature of travel.

The "Guide" and Its Audience.
What is "The Essential Guide to a Life of Travel"?

First, let me being by explaining what "The Essential Guide to a Life of Travel" is not.

- It is not a book about how to travel on a shoestring. While I discuss costs and fees, the guide does not focus on the finance of travel.
- It is not a book about trips or tours, such as what you find in a travel agency book.
- It is not a book about travel in the United States.

Rather, "The Essential Guide of a Life of Travel" attempts to provide everything you need to know to travel abroad, outside the United States. It is aimed at assisting all travelers, from those who only dream of travel to those who venture out frequently. And, because I am a solo traveler, I also include useful information for traveling alone.

Maybe you think you want to travel, but don't know how to begin or are generally fearful. This book is an excellent reference for you.

Perhaps you are a frequent traveler. But, you have limited yourself to tours and now you want to get a more in-depth experience in a city, country or region. This book is an excellent reference for you.

Of course, it is impossible to include everything there is to know, especially as more, new, and changing information emerges. If I waited to include the all up-and-coming information, I would never finish. However, to attempt to alleviate that conundrum, I include links to everything I discuss within the discussions and also in Appendices B and C, providing the resources for you to explore and research beyond the covers of this Guide.

You can see from the Table of Contents, I attempt to be comprehensive and detailed within the variety of topics. It's a lot of information and can be overwhelming. To avoid your getting bogged down, I include a "check lists" in CHAPTER Thirteen: Putting It All Together.

And, to pique your interest in travel, beyond the details and facts, I include a series of vignettes throughout these pages. The word "vignette" comes from the French *vigne*, meaning "little vine." The term specifically arose from the small vines drawn on the pages of printed texts. My stories, impressions, or vines are meant to entangle your imagination and entice you to travel.

I hope you find this book both useful and entertaining. I also hope you enjoy reading and using the "The Essential Guide to a Life of Travel" as much as I enjoyed writing it.

TABLE OF CONTENTS

Endorsements   iii
Dedication   iv
Introduction   v
"The Guide" and its Audience   viii
Acknowledgements   xiii

CHAPTER One: Transportation   1
  Travel by Plane   2
  Travel by Train and Bus   6
  Ferries   7
    Local Transportation   9
  Vignette: The Feve   10

CHAPTER Two: Lodging   15
  Booking Websites   16
    Hostels   17
    Housesitting   25
    House Swapping   30
    Couchsurfing   32
  Vignette: WIFI Promises and Challenges   33

CHAPTER Three: Insurance   35
    Non-emergency related needs   36
    Travel Medical Insurance   36
    Trip Insurance   36
    Where to Start   36
  Emergency Medical Reunion Insurance   41
  Trip Cancellation and Lost Luggage   42

CHAPTER Four: Passports and Visas   44
    Passports   44
    Visa Requirements   46
    The Schengen Area   46
  Vignette: Puccini in Lucca   51

CHAPTER Five: Banking, Debit Cards,
         and Frequent Flyer Credit Cards   54
  Banking and Debit Cards   54
  Frequent Flyer/Points Credit Cards   55

CHAPTER Six: Communication   58
  Cell Phone Options   59
  Other Ways to Communicate   61
  Battery Pack   62
    Keeping up with U.S. News   63
  Vignette: Barga, Italy   64

CHAPTER Seven: Travel Apps   67
  Essential Apps   68
  Useful Apps   73
  Nice-to-Have Apps   75
  Vignette: Cusco, Peru   76

CHAPTER Eight: Safety   78
  U.S. Department of State: Worldwide Caution   79
    U.S. Department of State: STEP Program   82
    Keep Documents Safe and Accessible   82
    Cell Phone Safety Tips   85
    Personal Safety   86
      Guidelines   88
  Vignette: Prague   93

CHAPTER Nine: Healthy Travel   93
  Guidelines for Healthy Travel   93
  Exercise Apps   99

CHAPTER Ten: Luggage and Contents   102
  Carry-On Luggage Requirements
        for International Flights   102
  Checked Baggage Requirements
        for International Flights   104
  Now, you have asked me....   105
  Vignette: San Sebastián   110

CHAPTER Eleven:
      Multiple Destination Trip Planning   113
  Useful Websites for a Multi-City Trip   113
  When to Go: Know Your Seasons   114
  Travel Overland, by Train or Bus   117
  Hub Cities   117
  Vignette: Fez, Morocco   118

CHAPTER Twelve: Miscellaneous and Odds and Ends   121
  Immunizations   121
  Driver Safety Abroad   124
  International Driving Permits   124
  Rental Car Insurance   125
  Vignette: Krakow: A Capitulation   127

CHAPTER Thirteen: Putting It All Together   125
  Pre-Planning Checklist   125
  Essential Items Checklist   127

CHAPTER Fourteen: Final Thoughts   137

APPENDICES   139
  A. Definitions   140
  B. Sources and Resources   141
  C. Websites: Explore Destinations   143
  D. Disclaimer   144

INDEX   145

About the Author   159

ACKNOWLEDGMENTS

Nothing of significance is ever done well without the help of many others. My colleagues and friends prodded, pushed, encouraged, and challenged me all along the way. I'm grateful and honored. I appreciate those who took the time to write glowing endorsements.

I especially am thankful to Enis Dibrani, whose beautiful cover design captured the essence of this book; to Elion Misini, whose positive attitude and inquisitive mind always inspire me to reach higher; to the sweet, lovely, and intelligent Lavdije Pllana, who is a great friend; and, to the incorrigible Hasan Salihu, who always finds an easy answer to what seems an insurmountable challenge. Finally, a special acknowledgement to Dr. Sharon Hart and Steve West who welcomed me to Prishtina with open arms and made it possible for me to come to know the wonderful people of Kosovo.

CHAPTER ONE

Transportation

Introduction
Travel by Plane
    How I Use Booking Sites
    Three important notes
        AirFareWatchDog
        Airteck
        Google Flights
        Hipmunk
        Momondo.com
        Sky Scanner
Two Unique Booking Websites: Flynous and Secret Flying
Travel by Train and Bus
Ferries
Rome2Rio and The Man in Seat Sixty-One
Local Transportation

Introduction

This is the exciting part of planning a trip. That is, digging through and researching the possibilities. Yet, it can also be the most confusing, especially in the early stages of the planning process.

Usually, I decide where I want to go and stick with that; but, sometimes I'm drawn away from my initial destination when I see beautiful photos on websites like The Lonely Planet or Conde Nast Traveler or see video ads highlighting the colorful scenery and intriguing cultures of places like India, Thailand, or Africa.

Furthermore, I get carried away when I read travel blogs or hear my friends' stores about their adventures. There is so much to see and learn!

Whatever your decision –making process is, when you finally landed on a destination, the real work begins. Usually, transportation preferences is the first step because it's often the most expensive portion. Unless you love analyzing minutia, it can be a daunting task to ferret out timelines, routes, and expense.

This Chapter provides a list of booking websites that will meet your particular transportation needs, from planes and trains to ferries and local transportation.

Travel by Plane

If you have done any research online to find flights, there are websites galore. And, more keep popping up every day. Of course, I can't list them all in this book.

Therefore, what I have listed here are my favorite websites, in alphabetical order. Like you, I have my own specific interests. For example, I intensely dislike sites that cluttered the page with pop up's from other sites. First, I'm overwhelmed and then, when I have looked closely at the so-called savings, I do not find any significant difference. As a result, I don't want to be bothered. I always go back to my favorites.

The sites that I have included below work for me. I find them user-friendly, include the "bells and whistles" that are useful to me and they are reliable. And, because I have used them so often, I'm familiar. I know where to go and what to look for. Perhaps you have your favorites, too. If you find sites new to you in this listing, I encourage you to spend some time to see how they work. Become familiar. See what fits your particular needs.

How I Use Booking Sites

After I find the best flight and before I book, I go to the airline website and go through these steps:

1. I look for a cheaper flight. I have found, on occasion, slightly cheaper flights and/or a better time.

2. I look for any frequent flyer associations. I always join. Usually, it is free, but sometimes there is a charge, such as with Wizz Air. With Wizz Air, the charge for the association provides you a discount on fares, luggage allowances, preferential seating, etc. The savings is a wash but it's worth consideration, especially if you think you will use Wizz frequently.

3. I check the baggage allowances.

4. I check for any hidden fees, such as fees: seat assignment, food, check-in, etc.

Three important notes before we begin:

1. I encourage you to avoid using your debit card to purchase airline tickets. Even if your debit card has a Visa or MasterCard logo, if the airline cancels your flight or goes out of business, you cannot expect the same protections you enjoy with an American Express, Visa or MasterCard credit account.
2. I encourage you to avoid U.S.-based booking sites for international transportation simply because often they do not include many of the international airlines.
3. Some of the flight booking websites listed below are not limited to flights, and include other modes of transportation, as well as lodging and tours. However, for the purpose of this Chapter, I focus only on transportation.

AirFareWatchDog is helps you search through thousands of airfares. The best benefit is the fare alert. It also has a very useful newsletter that focuses on travel sites and tips.
www.airfarewatchdog.com

Airtrek is a leader in multi-stop international flight, especially complex routes with up to 25 stops! This is the go-to site if you want to travel around the world. Get first-hand person-to-person assistance by phone for business travel and group trips. Also, Airtrek has an automated Trip Planner...a great feature when planning for at least three stops internationally in at least two countries, not including the start and end cities. Use "Trip Planner," key in information to find a combination of flights and stops you like.

Submit your choices and an Airtrek consultant contacts you with details and prices. They book the flights and you are on your way! (While the site doesn't list lodging, they provide do consultants who provide recommendations.) www.airtreks.com

Google Flights has excellent features and is the big buzz at the time of this writing with all its new bells and whistles. While I mention in the notes above to avoid U.S.-based booking sites, this may be the exception. Google Flights is worth consideration. Benefits include the abilities to search from up to five departures to five destinations at once, track fares and learn about their patterns with visual timeline graphs. Access local pricing* and potentially save extra bucks on your ticket. Compare amenities and legroom without have to browse around. Finally, track fares and learn patterns with Visual Timeline Graphs. Also, get alerts via email. www.google.com/flights

---

*I discuss Virtual Private Networks (VPN) in Chapter Seven. However, more specifically and useful for this Chapter, having your own VPN allows you to play with your "online location". For example, even though you may be in New York this morning, seeing flight prices in dollars, you could turn your VPN on to the UK and be quoted prices in British Pounds. For many flights this won't make much difference, but for some you'll actually find real savings for booking in one currency versus another. Norwegian Airlines and flights within Asia are prime examples where this occurs.

Hipmunk offers comprehensive travel search, from commercial flights, trains, and charter flights to hotels and vacation rentals through Airbnb. The website, mobile app, and artificial intelligence (AI)--powered bots used with the Virtual Travel Assistant help save time and money by comparing top travel sites to show the perfect flight or hotel at the cheapest price.

(What is an AI-powered bot? It is a computer program which conducts a conversation via auditory or textual methods. See Appendix A: Definitions.)

Momondo.com is a global travel search site that makes it easy to compare the prices on flights and travel deals. And when ready to book, the site directs you to the relevant company. Momondo, as other sites on this list, is a booking site and doesn't sell the tickets.

Frankly, Momondo is my go-to booking site. What I like about Momondo is:

- It's geared for worldwide travel and therefore connects to all airline booking agencies, big and small.
- It includes small airline companies that are often not included on the larger sites.
- It provides a vertical bar chart with dates to compare prices, similar to Google Flights. (See above.) You can see immediately when to schedule a cheaper flight, rather than repeatedly, *ad nauseam*, typing in one date at a time...or even a three-day spread, to find a better price.

SkyScanner is very good and includes most all the benefits with all these companies. Some people swear by SkyScanner, especially because of its travel alert system. www.skyscanner.net

Two Unique Booking Websites: Flynous and Secret Flying

Flynous and Secret Flying provide deals and tips for flights. What separates these from the rest is the process results. That is, when you key in a destination, the results are not an array flights. Rather, only special deals and promo codes emerge. As a result, these two sites can save you money and time because they have already researched and found the best deals. Furthermore, unlike the other sites noted above, Secret Flying and Flynous also list deals on "open jaw" and "error fares."

You may be asking yourself, what's an **open jaw**? Open jaw is a trip in which you fly to one destination and return from another

And, what is an **error fare**? An error fare is a reduced ticket price which comes as a result of human or computer mistake. The savings are incredible. I saw an error fare from Singapore to New York City for ninety-nine cents! Yes, less than a dollar. I assume someone or something failed to add the zeros! Ninety-nine cents was by far the lowest I've ever seen, but see it, I did!

However, a warning: if something seems unbelievable, perhaps it might be. Please read the details print when considering error fares. Both Flynous and Secret Flying explain flights such as these can be cancelled and go on to say how that might affect your decision making.

Flynous is focused on European flights; not flight within the United States. However, it does include deals to and from the U.S.A. Flynous provides deals hotels, as well. This site sends you directly to the airline or hotel rather than to a third party. www.flynous.com

Secret Flying is especially good if you can act quickly. Similar to the others, Secret Flying is not a travel agent or booking agent. Rather, it posts fare details and link to third-parties and you book yourself. What is exciting about this site is the variety of saving offers, including promo codes. Secret Flying also includes savings on hotels. www.secretflying.com

Travel by Train and Bus

You know, there is really no need to fly within Europe, especially in Western Europe. It's surprisingly easy, quick and comfortable to travel overland by train throughout virtually all countries. The challenge is finding out how to do it and where to buy tickets.

I have tried to book through the individual country's websites, like Renfe in Spain or Trenitalia in Italy, but I was not successful.
Honestly, I think it is because I didn't know enough details, such the variety of train stations in one city, their locations, even their names! And, without knowing the details, I just kept playing the foolish game of hit and miss! I confess, I missed more than I hit.

For example, I was trying my best on the Renfe (Spain) website to get from Salamanca to Gandia, via Madrid and Valencia. Welp, no matter what I tried putting data in those fields on the website, I came up with nothing. Ultimately, I walked to the train station in Salamanca and found that I had to take a bus to a different train station in Madrid to get to the Valencia station...the only Madrid station where I could catch a train to the Valencia station that would allow me to catch a train to Gandia. Just how in the world would I ever know that? If I knew everything...the names, the routes, the name of the routes, the stations and the names of the stations, I could easily use Renfe.

I needed to know what I didn't know! Of course, now I know. However, because I now know, I don't need to use the Renfe website. I can simply purchase the ticket at the train station BECAUSE I know what tickets to buy!

Ferries

Ah, doesn't traveling by ferry, over the oceans and seas sound romantic? So true! But beyond the romantic water and ocean and sea breezes, over water transportation it is less hassle and money than flying. It is certainly the way to go for island hopping in Greece or Croatia, and for overnight Scandinavian destinations.

And, many times you have the option of taking a ferry that includes car transport. These are great and in most any weather. On the other hand, smaller and speedier crafts called catamarans, only serve passengers, no automobiles. Note, also, because of their size, they have fewer seats and are more likely to have cancellations and/or schedule changes as a result of weather conditions.

Usually ferries are operated by a variety of smaller ferry companies. While you can access the schedules online, often they are posted what we Americans would call "late," a mere few days before the sailing season begins.

You know what I'm thinking? Let's take the mystery out of this mode of transportation, too. Go through Rome2Rio and/or The Man in Seat Sixty-One for clear and accurate information.

Rome2Rio and The Man in Seat Sixty-One

So, what is the answer? Because I never give up, I finally found the best, user-friendly websites that provides up-to-date, accurate and comprehensive information for train travel.

Rome2Rio: This is my favorite go-to website for transportation. (It is also an outstanding a good source when I am looking to travel within a region or country…and sometimes, within a city.) Rome2Rio is a simple, but comprehensive website, including flights, trains, buses, taxis, ferries/boats, and your own vehicle or rental car.

It allows you to see how to get from point A to point B via the best and cheapest way possible. Just enter your departure and arrival destinations and it will give you all the bus, train, plane, or boat routes that can get you there, as well as the costs. You can compare costs, how long each mode of travel takes, any lay overs or transfers, etc. Along with the estimated prices, it links directly to the transportation companies. It's easy to understand and navigate. And, frankly, when it comes to bus, I choose to go to Rome2Rio rather than trying to find bus companies with user-friendly websites, especially when I'm traveling through more than one country.

No need to try to find the right bus, from the correct location, etc. The times, dates, locations, etc. meeting the needs you have identified with Rome2Rio simply pop up! www.rome2rio.com

The Man in Seat Sixty-One: This one-man show has everything you ever wanted to know about train travel, not just in Europe, but all over the world. The Man, Mark Smith, has incredible knowledge. Furthermore, he has the ability to share his knowledge in an extremely user-friendly fashion.

His website tells you the best routes, train times and fares from London to major destinations all over Europe. It explains what the trains are like, and the best way to buy tickets.

It also explains the best routes, train times and fares for travel between the major cities of Europe, and how to buy the cheapest tickets, whether you live in the U.K., Europe, the U.S.A, and Australia, or wherever.

Why would I take up space trying to reinvent the wheel in this book when there's The Man? See for yourself at this link: **www.seat61.com**

Local Transportation

Finding local transportation can be daunting. I have used Uber (see Chapter Seven), taxis, subways, trams, and buses. How? First, I check Rome2Rio. If no luck, I ask the hotel concierge and locals. If

I'm not staying in a hotel, I step into a hotel and ask for information. I have never been turned away and always treated warmly.

Vignette: The Feve

I somehow accessed an informative article on the internet about traveling the northern coast of Spain, by train, by the Feve train, actually. This is a trip my physician back in the States raved about, although he drove a car and made no mention of any train. He insisted I explore the magnificent northern coast with cliffs, mountains, countryside, beaches, goats, cows, farm houses, tourist spots, little-known villages, and lovely, picturesque hamlets.

My British friends, John and Ann, who live in Spain, also brought this journey to my attention. They hadn't explained it themselves but had heard wonderful stories. Still, they knew little to nothing about the Feve.

Aw, the Universe was signaling me, again, and I simply had to follow this path.

John, Ann, and I began our research.

The Feve journey along the northern coast is found in Galacia, Spain, along 1030 miles of coastline on the Atlantic Ocean. This narrow-gauge train service runs along the rugged northern coast from Bilbao through Santander and Oviedo to León. It plunges through tunnels, up steep inclines, creaks around curves, and stops at lots of places – but only when would-be passengers wave to the conductor to stop the train so they can board.

This area of Spain, the northern coast, is a popular vacation area for the Spanish. It's safe to say that few tourists have taken this Feve journey on their own. Most tour with travel companies.

I was intrigued with a four-day tour from Bilbao to La Coruna for over $4000! Imagine how fantastic that would be. I'm envisioning incredible high-end restaurants and hotels, with thick carpets, glass chandeliers, with doormen and staff impeccably dressed to the nines. The Galacian restaurants included in this tour must include the best wines. The Galacian cuisine is phenomenal and revered worldwide.

Yeah.

But, honestly, $1000 a day is way too steep me. I spent $4000 for a week in Paris. It was wonderful, but terrible guilt and ate at me for months. Naw, I want to get in the area, and I mean, IN the area…sit alongside the locals, eat at their favorite spots, drink their wines, learn about their families, listen to their stories.

And, no highfaluting tourist bus for me. Gimme the ancient Feve!

Allow me to digress and discuss the history of train tracks and train service in Spain. There were two: (1) initially called narrow-gauge and later named Feve (Ferrocarriles Españoles de Vía Estrecha) and (2) broader-gauge network named Renfe (Red Nacional de los Ferrocarriles Españoles).

The narrow-gauge railway transport was first developed in Northern Europe during the 19th century, spurred not only by rapid economic growth, but also by landscapes favorable to railway construction. In 1852 the first narrow-gauge line was built and, in 1863, a line reached the Portuguese border.

Meanwhile, Spain had decided, early on, to build additional railways at an unusual broad-track gauge (1.668 meters or 65.67 inches), reportedly to ensure incompatibility with France's railway, thereby hindering a French invasion; or, as noted in other records, to allow bigger engines to climb the steep passes in the second most mountainous country in Europe.

Apart from the widespread broad-gauge lines, a large system of narrow-gauge railways (1.006 meters or 39.6 inches) was built in the more mountainous parts of Spain, especially in the north coast of the country, where narrow gauge was the most adequate option.

In 1941, the Franco regime nationalized the broad-gauge network by forming the Renfe. Likewise, the narrow-gauge lines were all grouped together and finally nationalized in the 1950's. Hence, the Feve was born.

By 1965, the Feve organization started absorbing numerous private-owned narrow gauge railways. At the center of this system is a line which runs for 650 km (404 mi) along the entire length of Spain's north coast and, since 1982, it has connected cities of San Sebastián, Bilbao, Santander, Oviedo, to Ferrol. Also, there is a line from Bilbao, southwest, to León.

11

John, Ann and I updated our historical knowledge. Unfortunately, we were unsuccessful at finding an actual Feve website to find the stations, the trails, the schedule, the prices, or, just about anything! And, we were not successful going through the Renfe website to learn about Feve.

We determined the junkets through a variety of websites having little to do with Feve. John called every Tourist Center to access the Feve office at each stop, learning the duration and then, only, how to get to the next stop. No one had any more information beyond their own station and how to get to the next station. That is, the San Sebastián station clerk could tell us how to get from San Sebastián to Bilbao, but, nothing going beyond Bilbao. The clerks were able to tell us that, indeed, there was Feve service all along the Feve trail. But, no more.

Anyway, I never to choose to be the "ugly American." Rather, I embrace all cultures and forge ahead, learning to love whatever challenges I face.

The Renfe Company is responsible for Feve scheduling; therefore, one would think chatting with the Renfe clerks at the various train stations would reveal the actual Feve train junkets and schedules. Yes, one would think.

But, Renfe clerks know nothing about Feve or they feign ignorance. This is what I confronted during my excursion. However, as John found out and used to help me plan, the Tourist Offices, located at every Renfe train station, actually do know about Feve.

Alas, too often, information is incorrect and/or incomplete. And, note, Feve stations...often just an information window, are sometimes actually inside the Renfe station, but not always. Usually, I found Feve "offices" on the outside of the Renfe station buildings, maybe down some outside steps or just around the corner, some with large logos adorning the walls, some not.

Feve staff at the information/ticket counter speak little English and some, none. And, no, you cannot purchase a Feve ticket from a machine. You must buy your ticket from a live Spanish-speaking/non-English-speaking person!

Well, whose fault is that? It's not the Spanish. If you or I don't speak Spanish, we are the enemy of ourselves. Alas, fear not, I say!

To prepare, practice your "please's" (por favor) and "thank-you's" (gracias), be persistent and use lots of non-verbal language: Point to your watch, frown, to the schedule, shrug your shoulders, count on your fingers, fold your hands as if to pray for help, etc. And, whatever you do, if you are not clear, do NOT walk away. If you walk away, you can waste precious time, miss a connection, or, heaven forbid, be stranded. Be kind, patient and gently persistent. You can do it!

I left on the Renfe and traveled for a full twelve hours with four transfers from Gandia, to Valencia to Zaragosa to San Sebastián. I stayed for three days in San Sebastián and travelled west on the Feve, buying my tickets at each location to Bilbao, Santander, La Coruna, Loiba, and Ferrol.

My trip was fourteen days, from San Sebastián to La Coruna and I paid a total of $1,304 U.S.D...and that includes a seven-day retreat in Loiba at a fabulous apartment just steps from the Northern Cliffs of Spain. Cost for that week for $800. Subtract that from the total, now makes the cost of my Feve journey, a mere $504!

Each time, I bought my Feve ticket with the help of non-English speaking clerks. My Spanish improved and my confidence soared. I improved my ability to scamper quickly on and off each train.

Sounds easy enough until I had to consider traversing two to four narrow metal steps with rises ranging from 12 to 18 inches. I managed to scale up and down those steps with my guitar strapped to my medium size suitcase and a hefty backpack.

I would say I carried a full 70 pounds in total. I honed my skills and after two weeks, I had it down to a fine science!

But, best of all? I saw northern Spain in April before the trees filled with leaves. I had a clear view and the beauty of this country, the mountains, the valleys, the vineyards, the rivers and streams, the new-age windmills. And, of course, I met locals on the trains, in cafes, bars and restaurants. I met their families, listen to their stories and fell in love with new friends and another incredible region of Spain.

(Final note: Weeks after finishing my journey, I found the Feve link through Renfe. Don't know how we missed it, but we did!)

CHAPTER TWO

Lodging

Introduction
Booking Websites
Hostels
Introduction
      Why a hostel?
      How to find the perfect hostel for you.
      Packing for hostel stay
      Hostel Etiquette
      Unique Hostels
Housesitting
    Guidelines
House Swapping
Couchsurfing

Introduction

Lodging is the second most important and the lion-share of the cost of travel. To some, it may be the most important. In either case, where you spend the night, when you place your head on that pillow, where you shower or bathe, is of superior importance. According to your personal requirements and your tolerance level, this process requires a great attention to detail

I have listed what I consider the best booking websites below.

Yet, I have additional suggestions: When you land on a choice and before you book, go to the hotel website and compare prices to ensure you are getting the best price. Also, call the hotel and ask for a lower price. It's worked for me. And, actually, I have been encouraged by hotel personnel to book with the hotel rather than the booking site for the best price for future stays. If you want to save money, it's worth the time and effort.

The following pages address all sorts of lodging, including hotels, hostels, house sitting, house swapping and Couchsurfing.

(Although, many of the lodging booking websites listed below are not limited to lodging, and include flights, car rental, holiday packages, etc. However, for the purpose of this Chapter, I focus only on lodging.)

Booking Websites

Agoda focuses on lodging in Asia and is a "cousin" of Booking.com. (See below.) Great benefits include 24/7 customer service in 17 languages, guaranteed lowest price and refunds the difference if you find one lower, and join for free and access lodging at a thirty percent discount. www.agoda.com

Airbnb is an online marketplace and hospitality service, enabling people to lease or rent short-term lodging, including vacation rentals, apartment rentals, homestays, hostel beds, or hotel rooms. The company does not own any lodging; it is merely a broker and receives percentage service fees from both guests and hosts with every booking. It has over 3,000,000 lodging listings in 65,000 cities and 191 countries. The cost of lodging is set by the host.

Airbnb is by far my favorite. I enjoy staying in apartments where I can store perishables in the refrigerator and cook It's less expensive than hotels that are the same level of accommodation. I probably have stayed in over twenty apartments through Airbnb...so many that I feel like an expert. I recorded a podcast that explains all of the steps I go through to ensure the accommodations are exactly what I want. You can access that podcast on my YOUTUBE Channel: DiannAbroad or on my website. www.diannabroad.com/podcasts

BedandBreakfast.com focuses solely on offering B&B's throughout the world and includes everything from luxury bed and breakfasts to sprawling inns. www.bedandbreakfast.com

Booking.com is a travel fare aggregator website and travel metasearch engine for lodging reservations. The website lists over 1,400,000 properties in 226 countries and books 1,200,000 room nights per day. The site is available in 43 languages. Booking.com is ranked number one by Frommer's, sighting best prices for hotels under $200/night. www.booking.com

eDreams is an online travel agency that offers deals in regular and charter flights, low-cost airlines, hotels, car rental, dynamic packages, holiday packages and travel insurance within its localized sites across 33 countries and territories. www.edreams.com

Homeaway is a vacation rental marketplace with more than 2,000,000 vacation rentals in 190 countries. It has operated through 50 websites in 23 languages. The company offers a comprehensive selection of rentals for families and groups to find accommodations such as cabins, condos, castles, villas, barns and farm houses. It is a conglomerate and includes agencies such as VBRO, OwnersDirect, and Stayz, just to name a few. It was acquired by Expedia.com in 2015. www.homeaway.com

Homestay is exactly as it sounds. It provides accommodations in a local person's home while the person living in the house is away. I personally haven't used this but is recommended by many people, traveler's websites, and organizations. www.homestay.com

Trivago is similar to Booking.com. It is a lodging aggregator website and compares hotel prices. I find that the prices are too high for my budget. Frommer's rates Trivago rather low, just so you know. www.trivago.com

Hostels

Introduction
Why a hostel?

How to find the perfect hostel for you.
Packing for hostel stay
Hostel Etiquette
Unique Hostels.

Introduction

If you want to save money while traveling, consider staying in a hostel. I know what you are thinking: Hostels are not hotels. I have found that many people hate hostels. Some people wouldn't be caught dead in a hostel and shout, "For heaven's sake, what would the neighbors say!"

And then, some people love them and will be hostelers all their lives, regardless of their personal budgets.

The truth is, for a rock-bottom price of $12 to $40 a night, you get "no frills" accommodations in clean, stark dormitories. And many hostels have single rooms with private baths. Some also have a few doubles and some family rooms. It's a great way for couples and families to enjoy their privacy together, while saving money at the same time.

For students, travelers on a budget, solo travelers, groups or families who can take a whole room, and those hoping to meet other travelers, hostels can be a great option.

I stayed in a hostel in Quito, Ecuador. Honestly, I didn't realize I had reserved a hostel. When my taxi driver pulled up to my "hotel," I saw the La Rosita Hostel. My heart sank.
The difference between a hotel and a hostel is one letter, the letter "s." Well, that's not totally true, but I whispered that to myself as I was exiting the taxi. I knew that I reserved a single room with a private bath. Of course, I was worried what I might find.

The good news was, indeed, I had a single room with a private bath. Thank goodness! Yes, it was a sparse and small. But, it had two windows: one in the bedroom and one in the bathroom. Nice. Many hotels rooms don't have two windows.

It also had a large, flat-screen television; daily maid service with personnel dressed in all-white uniforms; and daily clean towels, bar soap, and shampoo. Plus, it was spotless, with gleaming tile floors. Named La Rosita, Spanish for rose, there were fresh roses in the lobby,
on the stairs, and in the halls, replaced weekly. Furthermore, the maids
helped me find a good 24-hour laundry service close by. A full load of laundry, washed, dried and neatly folded, was a mere $2.00.

I met a sweet, young couple from New Zealand. They had been backpacking throughout South America. If that wasn't romantic enough, Mark had proposed to Elaine at the top of Cusco, Peru a week before. They asked me to go out for sushi with them to celebrate. It was a great evening and we remain in touch. And, of course, I'm invited to the wedding!

I had planned to stay for one week, but I liked it so much, I extended my stay to a full month. Fee: $19/day!

Why a hostel?

First, hostels are very inexpensive with excellent breakfasts (usually included in the price). Second, because you are typically not alone in a room, there often is more time for conversation. You can easily get ideas, first hand, for local activities, transportation, and restaurants… including what people enjoyed most and least, what was worth the price of admission, what wasn't, and why. Also because hostels cater to budget travelers, guests are the best source of budget information on day tours and excursions.

How to Find a Hostel Perfect for You

Did you know that there official hostels, that is independent hostels and hostels belonging to a parent organization? First, a look at independent hostels.

Independent hostels. Independent hostels tend to be more free-spirited and colorful with fewer rules, if any. Of course, it follows that these types may not be as clean or organized. Also, unlike hostels belonging to a parent organization, independent hostels do not require a membership. In any case, it's worth doing a little research.

- If you are more interested in an independent hostel, start by looking for your perfect hostel by using any of the lodging suggestions starting on page 16. Generally speaking, when you access a comprehensive lodging site I have listed, you will find hostels among all the other lodging choices (hotels, B&B's, villa's, etc.) by choosing to view results of your search by price, from low to high. I would say, unless otherwise stated on the actual hostel site, the hostels that pop up are independent hostels.

- Hostel Bookers has access to hostels in over 3,500 destinations worldwide, for backpackers and student travelers, and everyone looking for great budget accommodation. www.hostelbookers.com

- And, for a wider net, google "hostels" and your destination. For example, type the following in the search field of your browser: "Hostels in Kotor, Albania." I was shocked at the number of hostels that emerged, including the oldest hostel in the world! Yes, and I saw it for myself in May of, 2017. It was lovely and booked solid!

Parent Organization for Hostels. These organizations have hundreds of hostels within their organization and also specific standards and guidelines for all aspects of running a hostels, such as, cleaning, booking, staffing requirements, etc.

Hostelling International (HI). HI began as a youth hostel service in the 30's and initially adhered to the hostels rules for young people, such as lockout during the day and curfew at night). But, today, the rules are much more flexible. HI is booking site that provides information for official hostels all over the world. Travelers of all walks of life rave about Hostelling International. You may want to consider purchasing a membership with HI. If you plan to spend at least six nights at official HI hostels, you'll save money if you buy a membership card before you go. There are a variety of membership from $28/year for full benefits, free if you're under 18 and $18 if you're 55 or over. Also, you can chose the $18 eMembership which doesn't include frills such as insurance and currency exchange. Nonmembers who want to stay at HI hostels can sometimes get an "international guest card" at their first hostel and pay about $5 extra per night. www.hihostels.com

STF Hostel is also a parent company with very unique hostels – no two are alike. There are STF hostels all over Sweden – even where you would least expect to find them. Often, they are housed in buildings with an interesting history, and a number of them are an adventure in their own right. So many hostels, too little time and space to list here; same goes for the prices. You simple must check it out for yourself. www.swedishouristassociation.com

Whether you choose to go independent or with a hostel belonging to a parent company, you need to do your homework to find the hostel perfect for you. Here's how.

1. After you have picked out a few of your favorite hostels, **check the location on a map** to how close it is to downtown, airport, train stations, historic districts, or other places of interest to you.

2. Go a step further and access the hostel on **Instant Google Street View** for visual details. www.instantstreetview.com

3. Again, go to my favorite site, **Rome2Rio.** (See Chapter One.) Find all forms of transportation: train, bus, taxi, etc. And, don't forget to check out the fees and the time it takes to get from one location to another.

4. Also, read the **reviews** carefully. Of course, there are great hostels out there; but, like anything else, you can find some seedy places, too. Take your time to ensure the hostel you have chosen meets your needs and your standards.

5. Don't be afraid to **call and/or email** and ask questions.

Packing for a Hostel Stay

Most people are good, honest people. But it never hurts to take special care when you are bunking in a room with strangers. All of your belongings should be in zippered, padlocked compartments of your bag. And, many hostels do not offer the typical amenities offered at hotels.

Knowing this, I suggest you add this following items to your packing list:

- your own toiletries (soap and shampoo),
- a padlock to lock your locker,
- flip flops or sandals for the shower,
- ear buds for your phone and computer,
- ear plugs if you are a light sleeper, and
- towels. (Some hostels do provide towel, but, check for sure.)

Hostel Etiquette

The general rule here is "Do unto others as you would have them do unto you." However, this topic deserves further attention.

- Make sure you are clean and tidy, in your space and especially in the bathroom.
- Keep the use of your space to a minimum. Be courteous to others' space.
- Respect others' privacy, even if they are just across the room.
- Be quiet at all times, especially if you have to leave early in the morning or you come home late at night.
- If you have to leave early in the morning, prepare for departure the night before to avoid waking others as you leave.
- Don't turn the light on when others are sleeping.
- Eat in the common room, not in your room. Besides the clutter, the smell of food can linger in a room for hours, even days.
- If you wear cologne, be aware of its potency. Consider avoiding cologne or asking your bunkmates if your cologne is disturbing to them.

Finally, be tolerant. Perhaps they have not had the benefit of reading this Guide and are unaware of hostel etiquette.

Unique Hostels

Maybe you can find your perfect spot in these little-known hostels.

Hostel Celica is in Ljubljana, the beautiful capital city of Slovenia. Once a prison, today it's one of the most interesting hostels in the world. For a century, this space separated people from the view of the incarcerated individual. After the prison was closed to inmates, artists occupied the buildings for 10 years. The artists "opened it for fresh channels of expression." It was opened to travelers in 2003. Today, it is a social center and an arena of different ideas and a refuge for travelers, artists and all people of good will. Hostel Celica is an exceptional example of how art can transform a space with a dark and difficult history into a space of open possibilities and positive vibrations.

Owners explain, "It does not matter who you are, what you believe in and whom you love, all travelers are welcomed in Celica, with no exception. The message of openness and reception is also a corner of peace... where travelers find time for a spiritual experience or simple reflection. There are six areas, each representing [each of the] five world religions (Christianity, Islam, Judaism, Buddhism and Hinduism). The sixth is empty, open to an unknown god, which can be found by everyone." Prices range from $22 - $33 a bunk a night. The photos are incredible. www.hostelcelica.com

Jumbo Stay. Yeah, stay overnight in an actual jumbo jet! Located at the Stockholm Arland Airport, just 5 – 10 minutes by shuttle to airport check-in. Prices begin at about $60/ night for two-bedroom dorm to $230/night for a Double Bed Suite. Jumbo Stay is not just a hostel, it's also an exciting place to go on an excursion for the whole family and for aviation enthusiasts.

Non-house guests are welcome to have a look inside the airplane and to learn its history. There is a café, where you can purchase breakfast, coffee, cookies, ice cream, sandwiches and warm meals. For the best view of the airplane and of the taxi-runway, you can walk along the left wing observation deck and experience the feeling of standing on top of a real wing of a jumbo jet. www.jumbostay.com

STF Hostel (a parent company). There are STF hostels all over Sweden – even where you would least expect to find them. Stay where you have the smell of seaweed and the sea outside your window, in the middle of a national park or in the city. Stay at a woodland cabin in the forest where you get to chop your own wood and fetch your own water. Or spend the night in a suite, deep in the underground, in what was once a mine. So many hostels, too little time and space to list here; same goes for the prices. Some hostels are as little as $40/night. You simple must check it out for yourself. www.swedishtouristassociation.com/learn/stay-stf-hostel

The Mountain Hostel. Ah, but what about an alpine hostel villa in the Swiss Alps? When The Mountain Hostel was built in 1563, it was occupied by two families which kept cows and goats in the basement and lived in the building above which was split into two. It remained a farming home for hundreds of years until 1939 when Lina Von Allmen converted the building to a hostel. By 1996, Petra and Walter took over the business and put their hearts and souls renovating into its current charming, yet modest, state.

Located in the heart of the UNESCO World Heritage Jungfrau region, The Mountain Hostel is "simply love at first sight." Buzzing with travelers from around the world, this hostel seems to attract a certain type of traveler – social, fun, respectful and adventurous type with a love for the natural beauty that the Alps provide. It's a great base for outdoor activities.

Petra and Walter describe The Mountain Hostel in this way: "The easygoing and fun environment at our hostel leads to memories and friends that last a lifetime. In the evenings you will find travelers playing cards and games, guitar and piano. It's amazing to see familiar faces that come back every year sitting side by side with new travelers in awe of the view, having a beer on the deck as the sun sets on the mountains.

The pictures on the website are breathtaking. Prices: as low as $40/night. Check it out! www.mountainhostel.com

Housesitting

Introduction
House Sitting and Pet Sitting
        Guidelines
House Swapping
Tips for the best house sitting experience

Introduction

House sitting is a growing travel trend that can be a fantastic win-win. It's a mutually beneficial system that matches travelers with homes. And often, matching animal-loving travelers with sweet creatures that need attention and love. House sitting is a good way to live like a local and experience the authentic. The options are endless: Spend a few months on an island. Stay at a castle in Europe. Live off-grid in the jungle.

House and Pet Sitting. There are house sitting locations all over the world. Yes, homes in virtually every country, and in a variety of locations, including in major cities, outside cities, and in rural and remote areas.

One of the greatest benefits of house sitting is free lodging! Yep, you pay nothing to stay in someone's home. But, of course, you typically are required to take care of animals and pets, clean the house, and handle maintenance issues and emergencies that occur…and perhaps more.

House sitting usually includes taking care of animals. If you enjoy animals and have the requisite experience, this is a great option for you. Most everyone likes dogs and cats. Dogs love to take walks which can allow you to explore local areas, such as parks and beaches. Sleep with puppies and kittens. Even more, feed, groom and ride horses! Milk goats and cows. Feed the chickens and collect eggs.

Length of stay is another benefit. Housesits can be as little as a few days to as long as six months to a year or more. Of course, longer stays allow you to get to know more about the surrounding area, mix with the locals, etc.

Before I introduce you to the various house sitting and pet sitting agencies, allow me to note that I have had quite a few experiences house and pet sitting. All have been extremely positive. However, it is important to note that I didn't not go through an agency for these gigs.

Rather, I asked friends I had come to know while traveling. My friends put me in touch with families who needed a sitter, and, of course,
vouched for my character. These families, by the way, were not registered with any house sitting agencies. I encourage you to consider letting people know you are available to house sit and pet sit when you know them well enough and feel confident you can trust them.

Listed below, in alphabetical order, are the most popular house sitting and pet sitting agencies. They all have a fee, of course. That is, in order to list yourself as a sitter, you must register, provide pertinent information, write an honest and glowing review of yourself, list your countries of preference, list your pets of preference, note times you are available, and pay a membership fee. Most agencies also require sitters to provide an official criminal background check which is easily processed through your State police agency for a fee of $25-$50.

To give you an idea of fees, TrustedHouseSitters seems to be the largest and the most expensive, although it was marketing a reduced rate from $119/year to $107/year at the time of this writing.

I encourage you to access these companies on the web to get all the details.

- HouseCarers   www.housecarers.com
- HouseSitMatch   www.housesitmatch.com
- House Sitting World   www.housesittingworld.com
- Mind My House   www.mindmyhouse.com
- Nomador   www.nomador.com

- TrustedHousesitters   www.trustedhousesitters.com

Guidelines

After you have found the perfect spot for your housesitting adventure and have an agreement, follow these guidelines.

1. Arrive a day early (or set up a meeting sometime in advance) to meet the homeowners and have them show you around. Questions may occur to you as you tour the property that wouldn't otherwise. It also provides an opportunity for them to show you little things that will make your life easier – where to find everything…how to manage the finicky vacuum, where and when to leave trash, etc.

2. Get instructions in advance. You will want to know details about the house, itself. For example, locking doors, checking on utilities, how to run appliances and who to call should a problem occur. If you have questions, make notes and discuss with the homeowners.

3. Determine in advance the rules around having guests, to ensure it is acceptable and under what conditions.

4. Get contact information for someone local to call in an emergency. What if you lock yourself out? What if something drastic happens and you suddenly have to return home?

5. Get all emergency information and keep it in one place, near the phone and/or computer. This will allow you to avoid searching in a crisis.

6. If caring for pets, clarify with the homeowners whether you are required to be with the pet every day. Also, if it is important to you, ask if it is possible to have someone sit for a day or two while you go to a class or exploring. Of course, you will want to limit to a minimum.

7. If housesitting includes the use of their car, ask about insurance, distances, type of gas and where to fuel up, and any unwritten quirky driving rules such as parking or places to avoid. (If you intend to drive, but sure to have acquired and have with your International Drivers' License. (See Chapter Twelve.)

8. Ask about "do's and don'ts." Is there a room or area of the house you are to avoid? Can you wear your shoes in the house?

9. Ask about food. Where is the nearest grocery store? Is food currently in the house available for you to eat? If they have a wine collection, what wines are off limits to you?

After your host family has departed:

10. Keep in touch. Send the homeowners an occasional email if they have asked for it, or are able to receive it. Send them photos of the animals so that they can see everyone is doing well.

11. Try to solve problems on your own with the instructions they have given. When and if you have a problem and you solve it totally, no need to bother them with it. If, however, the problem is a warning of things to come, such as overheated car or a boiler damage, keep them informed.

12. Be honest, of course, and don't do anything you wouldn't want the homeowner to find out about. Be especially cognizant of the animal rules. "No dogs on the bed" means no dogs on the bed.

13. Lock up when you leave the house, even if the owner don't typically lock up themselves. It is just smart.

14. Be smart and follow your own "be-safe" practices. For example, don't tell people where you are staying, even if they ask. If you have permission to use the car, obey the laws, including parking.

15. Take stock of the contents in the refrigerator and replace before the owners return. Ditto for the wine and alcohol.

16. Leave or send a thank you note after you leave. Either leave on the premises if outside the country or send in snail mail after your departure. It's so nice and much more personal than an email message.

I enjoy house sitting. It gives me some sense of normalcy which is a nice change. My most memorable experience was housesitting for five cats in a lovely house on Lake Erie while the owners went to England for six weeks. It was winter and the Lake was magnificent. The cats were easy and I loved sleeping with them.

I also took care of two beautiful dogs for a month in San Miguel de Allende, Mexico. The dogs required two walks a day. It was simple. While they were on leashes, they were the ones to walk ME to the park. And, you know, walking through the park with two lovely dogs is a great way to meet people.

I met the most interesting man…a writer who was working on an historical novel about a small community in Illinois. It was chock full of intrigue, fraud, murder and politics. We have kept in touch since then.

House Swapping

Remember the romantic comedy "The Holiday" with Jack Black, Kate Winslet, Edwards Burns, and Cameron Diaz? The character played by Diaz lives in California and the character played by Winslet lives in England. Both women, strangers to each other, find themselves in a crisis, eager to escape their troubles, and agree to swap houses for two weeks. (Great movie! I recommend it for all you romantics and Jack Black. He plays a romantic lead.)

This is the epitome of a successful home exchange. Of course, you don't have to be in crisis mode to take advantage of this cool way to go on a vacation!

Yet, you might think this is too much work. It is true, you are required to get your house "swap" ready, take pictures, and write an honest and glowing description of your house, the location, and the special benefits of staying at your place. You are also required to write a profile as a home owner, as well as a description of yourself as a visitor staying in someone's home.

When I worked to get my house "swap" ready when living on Amelia Island, Florida, I saw it as a good opportunity to get my home in order, spruce it up a bit. And, writing a description and the benefits of Amelia Island was easy with all the marketing already out there for this lovely location on the Atlantic Ocean. I fell in love with the Island all over again!

You might even think it too risky. Having perfect strangers stay in your house? Honestly, it occurs all the time, especially in Europe. Europeans are very open to inviting people to stay in their homes. It has happened to me many times. Furthermore, the profile and application process helps to weed out any riff raff.

While I never actually house swapped, I did meet someone, a writer, who wanted to finish her book and needed a quiet place to stay. I had planned a three-week trip to Greece and needed a pet sitter. Although, I didn't know her well, I felt like I could trust her. We struck a deal! And, of course, I introduced her to my neighbors and friends, not only to help her get acquainted locally, but also to let her know, subtly, that my friends would be around and perhaps, even watching. It was a win-win!

Go to each of these websites below and check out the "how to's."

HomeExchange	www.homeexchange.com
Home Link	www.homelink.org
Intervac	www.intervac-homeexchange.com

Couchsurfing

Couchsurfing is a network that lists millions of members who host fellow "surfers" in their homes for free. Most do this out of a sincere interest in meeting interesting people; many are in it for simply providing a free service to travelers in need and have actually couchsurfed themselves. They see it as "paying it forward."

If you are extremely tolerant, like to talk and listen, void of back ailments, don't have to have your very own pillow, and are looking for free lodging, this is the service for you. The majoring of people to take to this service are twenty-something solo travelers, but I have heard of older people and couples Couchsurfing.

While both travelers and Couchsurfing hosts are required to post their profiles on the website, safety remains a concern. I don't know of any statistics about safety issues; however, few people I know are open to sleeping on a stranger's couch for free. This implies little or no real privacy for the traveler or the host.

I would say a good tip for sleeping on the couch in a stranger's house is to be on the alert for creeps and scammers, especially if you are female.

Should you choose this service, as in any situation, be sure to have Plan B. Have another lodging location nearby and in your back pocket. Let plenty of people know where you are couchsurfing and even give them permission to call you, just to check in with you. Be sure to have your security call information handy on your phone. (See Chapter Eight.)

Finally, if, for some reason, you feel uneasy, trust your inner voice. Don't worry about offending anyone. Just depart the premises. www.couchsurfing.com

Vignette: WIFI Promises and Challenges

It all began January 15, 2016. Today, after nearly two years and over thirty countries, I have used a variety of websites to acquire lodging, including Airbnb, eDreams, Momondo, Booking.com, and more. Lodging hasn't been totally perfect, but by and large, the apartments and hotels descriptions have been true to form.

Yet, on occasion, I have been sorely disappointed with one aspect among the amenities: WIFI service. WIFI is of superior importance to me. It's not only my connection to the outside world, family, and friends, it also is a requirement for maintaining my website, writing blogs, and working on my books. I began to realize that when the list of amenities includes WIFI, it is silent on the quality of the WIFI service.

I ran into WIFI problems in San Sebastián, Spain, when I found that the hotel had WIFI but not all year around. Actually, it only had WIFI during the low season. When was I there? Of course, I was there during high season and no WIFI. Did the hotel description note WIFI was only available at low season? Of course not!

Another time, in Florence, Italy, I had a perfect apartment, easy walking distance along the Arno River to the shops at Ponte Vecchio. The apartment decor was right out of the 1950's, replete with old wooden kitchen cabinets painted a glossy dark green. The kitchen table had those cool metal legs. The table top, encircled with a strip of aluminum, was smooth plastic, printed with tiny red flowers. The cream chenille bedspread brought back memories of my bedroom in our Lindenwald neighborhood in Hamilton, Ohio. I loved this apartment. I felt like I was in old Italy.

On my first morning, like always, I accessed the internet to watch the latest news. The WIFI was fast and consistent. I connected with my VPN and was just about to view my bank account when the WIFI was lost. I assumed it was a momentary loss. But, after about 30 minutes, when I still didn't have access, I gave up, closed down my computer, and left for the day.

The next morning, I accessed WIFI again. It was a breeze. I decided to take a moment to email my host and tell her my WIFI experience the day before. She replied immediately noting that WIFI was available, but, for only an hour a day!

I went back and checked the Airbnb ad for this apartment, assuming I had missed this extremely important limitation to the WIFI. Well, of course, I found no reference to any time limit.

Needless to say, she received a very harsh review. And, from this moment on, I always email the host and hotels and question the quality of the WIFI. On some occasions, if I'm not convinced of their veracity, I have gone so far as to strike a deal: If I get there and the WIFI isn't strong as you say, the agreement is null and void. That minor effort has had excellent results.

Since I began my journey, I have come to know what is important to me and I always go through a process to check and recheck my priority areas to void getting stuck in an unpleasant situation. I'm proud of my fine-science approach to finding lodging.

Or so I thought.

CHAPTER THREE

Insurance

Introduction
Non-emergency related needs
Travel Medical Insurance
Trip Insurance
Where to start
    Credit Card vs. Travel Insurance Company
You decide to purchase travel insurance. Now what?
   Squaremouth
   Top rated providers for: families, solo travelers,
       adventurers, and long trips
   Roamright
   Insure My Trip
   World Nomads
Emergency Medical Reunion Insurance (EMR)
   Allianz Travel Insurance Deluxe Plan
   Roamright
   World Nomads
Trip Cancellation and Lost Luggage

Introduction

Travel insurance and health insurance are very confusing topics to parse. I think it is because most of the people talking about insurance are the insurance companies or travel sites, and I wonder about their motivation. Is it to provide important options, to get a cut of the action, or simply to make money? It was hard for me to know, until I sifted through the information from credible sources. This is an overview of what I learned:

1. **Non-emergency related needs**: If you need to see a doctor because you have a cold, minor but irritating intestinal problems, or a bad rash, there is no insurance coverage out there. You simply go to a pharmacist or a doctor and pay out of pocket. And, unlike the U.S., in most countries, these costs are minimal.

2. **Travel medical insurance** coverage while traveling outside the United States is available, but it is actually emergency medical insurance and does cover non-emergency problems, as noted above.

Travel medical insurance is for travelers who are leaving their home country and provides coverage for medical emergencies and evacuations. For example, (1) you fall and break a tooth or a leg or (2), your heart attack doesn't allow you to travel; or (3) you require transportation from a remote location to a proper medical facility.

Depending on the company selling it, travel medical insurance is sometimes called International Medical Insurance, International Travel Insurance, or Worldwide Medical Insurance.

3. **Trip Insurance** coverage has to do with your trip: your flight, luggage, loss or theft of travel gear, cameras, electronics, etc.

Trip insurance covers trip cancellation, interruption, delay, baggage coverage, loss of camera or computer, etc. The fee is usually around 4 to 10 percent of the insured trip cost. The trip cost is based on age, trip length, and coverage amount.

Where to Start

First, check with your current health care carrier. Does your coverage apply to healthcare outside the U.S.? If not, see if you can get a rider for your trip. Call for all details and options.

If you are on Medicare, you probably are aware that Medicare does not cover you outside the U.S... However, your supplemental plan may indeed cover you.

My supplemental plan covers me for emergencies, any place in the world. Of course, I pay up front and then submit a claim for reimbursement.

Take the time to call the company that provides your Supplemental Plan Coverage, rather than sifting through endless pages trying to decipher the legal jargon. Get all the details about your coverage and discuss any special medical needs you may have. Be sure to ask which countries are NOT included in your coverage. Also, get contact information about the representative with whom you are speaking and request he/she email you copies of pertinent information. This way, you have a record and a contact for any future reference.

Complimentary Credit Card Coverage
Vs.
Travel Insurance Company Coverage

Credit card companies love to trumpet the "free" bonuses that come with their cards, especially the gold, platinum, and diamond cards. Some of these premium cards come with complimentary travel insurance, provided you meet certain criteria.

Using a credit card is so much easier than digging around trying to find insurance for every trip you take. Aha, but, which is better? Credit card insurance or insurance offered by travel insurance companies?

First, a few preliminaries about credit cards:

Free doesn't really mean free, of course, because you pay an annual fee for your credit card. The lower the fee, the less coverage and vice versa.

Obviously, you have to use the card to buy your departure ticket (or tickets, if you're travelling with your family) to be covered. Often there are also a minimum amount (typically around $500) per person you must spend/charge have to spend before departure on travel costs to activate coverage. But, you're going to spend that money on airfares and hotels anyway, right? So why not just put it on the card and not have to worry about taking out travel insurance?

A cursory view of credit card complimentary insurance policies might make credit card insurance look as good as or even better than coverage provided by insurance companies. However, there are differences worth exploring.

Finally, two very important preliminary notes:

1. Credit card insurance doesn't apply to domestic travel. Although some cards will reimburse expenses associated with domestic flight delays and missed connections.

2. If you use frequent flyer miles to purchase a flight and pay just the fee with your credit card, usually you are not eligible to use the credit card insurance.

The **not-so-good news** about complimentary credit card insurance:

- You need to use your credit card to buy your tickets and that usually means roundtrip tickets.

- To get complete coverage, beyond basic emergency medical treatment, some banks offering the credit card require you to notify them to activate extra features, such as property damage or luggage delays.

- Did you know that travel insurance companies charge about $100 just to file a claim? Well, credit cards top that and charge $250 or more per claim.

- Some credit card insurance does not automatically cover pre-existing conditions, and won't let you pay an extra premium for an exception. Those that do cover pre-existing conditions list them in their product disclosure statements. And, be aware that mental health is often not included under the definition of pre-existing conditions.

- If you're 80, you probably are not covered by your credit card insurance. And even if you're younger, if you have to interrupt your trip to go home because of a family member's death or illness, you're not even covered if the family member is are over 80. While travel insurance companies have age limits as well, there are companies that provide such insurance at a higher premium. However, some companies actually do cater to seniors.

The **good news** about complementary credit card insurance:

- While credit card insurance is complimentary, it is all relative. That is, the higher the annual fee you pay, the more coverage. Yet, these higher annual fees are still usually less than the premiums for travel insurance companies, but not always. That is to say, if you travel abroad once a year, the return on your annual fee investment is probably at a loss.

  However, traveling more than once a year yields a high return on investment, depending on the how much money you spend on your trips.

- Cards that come with travel insurance usually also come with point and/or frequent flyer miles. Therefore, travel insurance is a real perk.

- When you purchase from a travel insurance company, you are typically required to purchase a separate policy for each location. For example, if you plan an open jaw or an around-the world trip, you will be required to purchase insurance for each destination. This is not the case with credit card insurance.

Just as I have repeated throughout this guide, if you decide to apply for a new credit card that meets your travel needs, always read the fine print to make sure this is the product for you.

You decide to purchase travel insurance. Now what?

There are a multitude of companies out there. For easy access to a variety of travel insurance companies, so **Squaremouth** where you can you can search, compare, and purchase travel insurance from every major provider in the United States for international travel. www.Squaremouth.com

Check out these top-rated providers, listed specific to client needs:

Travel Insurance Providers	Client Categories
Travelex www.travelexinsurance.com	For Families
John Hancock www.johnhancocktravel.com	For Solo Travelers
IMG https://www.imglobal.com	For Adventurers
Allianz www.allianztravelinsurance.com	For Long Trips

And, I have seen companies that seem always to bubble to the top and are touted by travel companies and travel gurus

Roamright has a five star rating. I found this company through Squaremouth and checked it out for myself. I found excellent coverage (for both travel medical insurance and trip insurance). In order to get a quote, I said I would be taking 10 trips a year with each trip limited to 30 days. They quoted $192/month for complete coverage. That is by far the best quote with comparable coverage I have ever found for my particular needs.

Insure My Trip: If you're a senior, over 69, explore Insure My Trip. Insure My Trip serves as a broker for insurance companies and offers the best coverage and prices for older travelers. With their quote process, you can compare benefits, get quotes, buy policies, and save from the top-rated carriers. www.insuremytrip.com

World Nomads has a great reputation and is affiliated with Lonely Planet. Simple and flexible, they reportedly have great customer service. Note, if you are over 69, you can buy a policy, but it's bloody expensive. www.worldnomads.com

Final and important notes: Check coverage regarding dental and vision. Further, to make sure you are comparing apples to apples, check the "glossary of terms" for any insurance company you are considering. Especially review these terms: domestic partner, financial solvency, injury, medically necessary, natural disaster, preexisting condition, traveling companion, trip, etc.

Emergency Medical Reunion (EMR)

EMR is an important consideration, especially if you are a solo traveler. It's worth considering, in any case.

EMR is offered by many policies, however, the terms can vary greatly. If you chose to talk with World Nomads and/or Insure My Trip, be sure you know the exact terms of the insurance you're considering so that you can make a proper comparison between companies. Of course, this goes for any and all companies you contact, not just the ones I have listed here.

Here are three plans that are recommended by many knowledgeable travel authorities:

The **Allianz Travel Insurance Deluxe Plan** and above. Allianz explains, "If you're told you will be hospitalized for more than seven

days during your trip, we'll transport a friend or family member to stay with you. We'll arrange and pay for round-trip transportation in economy class on a common carrier."
www.allianztravelinsurance.com

Roamright seems to provide everything anyone would ever want. And, you can pick and choose. Important for this discussion, Roamright says, "When you are hospitalized for more than 7 days, the company will arrange and pay for round-trip economy class transportation for one individual selected by you from your home country to the location where you are hospitalized and return to the current home country. The benefits payable will include: The cost of a round trip economy air fare up to the maximum stated in your schedule of coverage and service emergency medical reunion. The period of emergency medical reunion is not to exceed 30 days, including travel." www.roamright.com

World Nomads, for those under 69 years of age: $1,500 in coverage. "If you're traveling alone and are admitted to hospital for 3 days or more, we'll arrange for someone to be with you and pay for their return economy airfare, accommodation, meals, essential calls and taxis of $150 per day for a maximum of 10 days." www.worldnomads.com

Trip Cancellation and Lost Luggage Insurance

As discussed above, you need both travel medical insurance and trip insurance. If your chosen provider doesn't include trip insurance, you need to explore that option with other companies to acquire this important coverage.

Check your credit card companies to review the complimentary trip cancellation and lost luggage coverage offered to you when you purchase tickets with your credit card.

This type of travel insurance can be confusing due to the lack of consistencies across countries. Therefore, be sure to read closely the policies, exclusions...all the fine print. Specifically, you want to know:

- What are the trip cancellation situations for which you are covered? Would you be covered if severe weather affected your trip and unforeseen circumstances such as, loss of funds or rescheduled business meeting called you away?

- Check on the details of trip cancellation and the variety of purchase options.

- What their policy is regarding gear? Before you leave for your adventure, use your cell phone to take photos of all your equipment, computer, camera, etc., to prove ownership, quality, and replacement costs.

CHAPTER FOUR

Passports and Visas

Introduction
Passports
REAL ID Compliant Driver's Licenses
Visa Requirements to Enter Foreign Countries
The Schengen Area
The European Union
U.S. citizens and the Schengen Area
Non-Schengen Area Countries

Introduction

Some of this information is this section is straight forward. Simply, you must have a passport to exit the United States and enter another country. However; given the recent changes in immigration attitudes, policies and laws, it is prudent to stay abreast of any potential changes. This Chapter explains how and where to keep up to date, and the complexities of the Schengen Area, listing both Schengen Area countries and non-Schengen Area countries.

Passports

The U.S. Department of State is the agency where all passport information is found. Whether you are renewing a passport or applying for the first time, you can fill out the proper form online. Applying for a U.S. Passport demand is on the rise and the Department of State expects to see 20 million applications in Fiscal

Year 2017. It is best to apply early and to take advantage of lower wait times September through December. For adults renewing their passport, the process can be done by mail.

For information on how to apply for a U.S. passport, go to travel.state.gov or call the National Passport Information Center toll-free at 1-877-487-2778/1-888-874-7793 (TTY/TTD).

REAL ID Compliant Driver's Licenses*

As I mentioned in the introduction to this Chapter, changes are running rampant. Specifically, beginning on January 22, 2018, domestic air passengers with driver's licenses issued by a state that is not yet compliant with REAL ID and that has not received an extension will need to show an alternative form of acceptable identification for domestic air travel. Both the U.S. passport card and passport book are REAL ID compliant. If you already have a REAL ID compliant driver's license, it will remain valid for <u>domestic</u> air travel.

What are the REAL ID Requirements?

The REAL ID Act, which became law in 2005, requires driver's licenses to meet minimum security standards for issuance and production. For air travel and certain other purposes, federal agencies are prohibited from accepting driver's licenses and identification cards from states not meeting the Act's minimum standards unless those states have been granted extensions.

The U.S. passport book and the U.S. passport card are REAL ID compliant and are acceptable identification to board <u>domestic</u> flights. The U.S. passport card is the same size as a driver's license and only costs $55 for first time applicants or $30 for those who have already had a passport. A U.S. passport book is always required for <u>international</u> air travel – passport cards are not valid for international air travel.

To find out if your state's driver's license or ID are Real ID compliant visit the Department of Homeland Security's website dhs.gov/real-id

*Source: www.state.gov/r/pa/prs/ps/2017/08/273747.htm

Visa Requirements to Enter Foreign Countries

Visa requirements to enter foreign countries are not complicated; however, there are too many countries to list here. However, The U.S. Department of State provides Country Specific Information for every country of the world. You will find the location of the U.S. embassy and any consular offices, information about whether you need a visa, crime and security information, health and medical considerations, drug penalties, localized hot spots and more. This is a good place to start learning visa requirements for your country destination(s).
www.travel.state.gov/content/passports/en/country.html

The Schengen Area

Schengen Area, named after "the Schengen Agreement" and established in 1995, is a policy of the European Union and signifies a zone where 26 different European nations acknowledged the abolishment of their internal borders with other member nations and outside. The Agreement allows for the free and unrestricted movement of people, goods, services, and capital, in harmony with common rules for controlling external borders and fighting criminality.

Through Schengen Area, borders between European countries are only existent on maps. Passport checks and border control passages are not required and gives the freedom of travel within and outside the Area is guaranteed, as if all 26 countries were one. Every country within the 26 countries in the Area share the common travel and movement rights.

The Schengen Area Member States:

Austria	Belgium	Czech Republic
Denmark	Estonia	Finland
France	Germany	Greece
Hungary	Iceland	Italy
Latvia	Lithuania	Luxembourg
Malta	Netherlands	Norway
Poland	Portugal	Slovakia
Slovenia	Spain	Sweden
Switzerland	Liechtenstein	

Note some additional information:

Three of the following European countries are associated members of the Schengen Area but are not members of the European Union: Iceland, Norway, and Switzerland.

Although France is a Schengen Area country, it did for some time, during heightened terrorists attacks within its borders, chose to institute border crossings and security checks.

Three of the following territories are special members of the European Union and part of the Schengen Area, even that they are located outside the European continent: the Azores, Madeira, and the Canary Islands. On the other hand, three of the following countries have open their borders with, but are not members of the Schengen Area: Monaco, San Marino, and Vatican City.

There are six more European Union members, that have not yet joined Schengen Area: Ireland and United Kingdom— that still maintain opt-outs and Romania, Bulgaria, Croatia, and Cyprus — that are required to and are seeking to join, at the time of this writing.

The European Union

Although most of the Schengen countries are in the European Union (EU), you should not confuse the Schengen Area with the EU. The EU consists of 28 countries.

Austria	Belgium	Bulgaria	Croatia
Cyprus	Czech Republic	Denmark	Estonia
Finland	France	Germany	Greece
Hungary	Ireland	Italy	Latvia
Lithuania	Luxembourg	Malta	Netherlands
Poland	Portugal	Romania	Slovakia
Slovenia	Spain	Sweden	United Kingdom*

*At the time of this writing, the Brexit (a term for the potential or hypothetical departure of the United Kingdom from the European Union.) was passed, occurred, and the United Kingdom had begun the process of leaving the EU. However, the exit from the EU is not yet complete.

U.S. citizens and the Schengen Area

While U.S. citizens do not need a Schengen Visa to enter and stay in the Schengen Area, there are restrictions with regard to length of stay:

U.S. citizens are not allowed to reside in the Schengen area beyond 90 days without any other legal permission. They are, again, a variety of legal permission. Please access this website to learn more: www.schengenvisainfo.com/who-needs-schengen-visa

The amount of days permitted to stay in any of the Schengen zone countries doesn't exceed 90 days/ three months every half a year, needless of the travel reasons. Translated, that means U.S. citizens can only reside in the Schengen Area for a total of 90 days. After 90 days, citizens are required to leave the Schengen Area. Furthermore, citizens are not permitted to return to the Area for a full 90 days.

It's that simple. However, if you want reside in the Area for less than 90 days…say 60 days…leave and return, you are permitted to do so. However, in this example, when you return, the first day you enter the Area, that day is number 61. Subsequently, you are permitted to remain for only for 29 days and you must exit the Area on the 90th day. (That is, 61 days plus 29 days equals 90 days.) Then, you are required to stay outside the Area for at least 90 days before you can return.

When you exit, the Area, you are required to pass through security and border patrol. If you have exceeded your 90 days, you will be allowed to leave, of course, but you will be fined. How much? It depends. Remember, you are in Europe…not the U.S.A. The fee can be a moving target.

Although I am not sure, I think it is possible that a note will be recorded in your passport file. If that is true, you may face additional problems in the future. I suggest you follow policy.

To make sure you are clear about the Schengen Area and your travel dates, please go to this website that provides a calculator which will make this all perfectly clear and accurate for your planning: https://ec.europa.eu/assets/home/visa-calculator/calculator.htm

Non-Schengen Area Countries

Obviously, you cannot cross borders from country to country outside the Schengen Area without going through border control. Actually, you must pass through border patrol when leaving a country and also when entering a country…every country, all over the world.

Unlike the lack of visa requirements for U.S. citizens traveling to the Schengen Area, other countries, but not all countries, require visas and the length of stay can vary from 15 days to 90 days. Furthermore, some countries require you to pay a fee and also acquire a visa weeks before your arrival. Please check the website of your country of origin for visa requirements: https://passportinfo.com

I suggest U.S. citizens also access the U.S. Department of State: www.state.gov/travel

Finally, be sure to check back often for any changes. And/or you can sign up for email updates.

Vignette: Puccini in Lucca

Again, the Universe was calling me. And, as always, I listened and found myself drawn to Lucca, Italy, the birthplace of Puccini, the Italian opera composer known as "the greatest composer of Italian opera after Verdi". Puccini was born Giacomo Antonio Domenico Michele Secondo Maria Puccini in 1858. Since the 1730's, his family had been tightly interwoven with the musical life of this city, providing five generations of organists and composers to the Cathedral of San Martino, Lucca's religious heart.

I had some knowledge about classical music and opera because I played French horn in the school orchestra from seventh grade to my senior year of high school. Although Puccini did not include sections for French horn in this compositions, we played Bach, Beethoven, Brahms and Strauss. I learned to love this music.

I had not had the privilege of attending a classical concert in a few years and Lucca had a Puccini concert nightly in the San Giovanni Basilique, just a brief walk from my apartment.

Actually, my lovely Airbnb apartment had been a convent, 600 years ago, and still had the original massive steel door and coved, red brick ceiling. It was a perfect perch on the second floor, with a large window, overlooking the food market and shops on the narrow street below.

I bought a concert ticket online for a mere fifteen euros and scurried to the church, arriving just a few minutes before curtain. The sight of the rows of simple folding chairs was disappointing at first because I wanted to see. Without risers, I would have to crane my neck around the heads in front of me just to get a partial view.

I rushed to the front and peeked around a crowd of white-haired couples looking to find the best seats when I sat a single open chair in the very front row. Quickly, I motioned to the gentleman sitting next to the vacant chair, signaling him to confirm that the chair was available. He smiled, nodded, and immediately placed his hand on the seat to save it for me.

I whisked passed the couples still in decision mode, sat down quickly, with a simple nod to my gentleman neighbor, and readied myself for what I knew was

51

going to be a fascinating ninety minutes. I faced a simple, slightly raised black platform, with a gleaming black grand piano.

At that moment, pianist Diego Fiorini, a gorgeous, young man with black wavy hair and perfectly groomed moustache, in a pristine tuxedo, came from behind the black curtain. The applause began. Like a graceful dancer, he entered on to the stage, stopped for momentary bow, moved around to the piano bench, flipped his tux tails, and sat. The audience hushed.

He began with Puccini's Intermezzo from "Manon Lescaut." The delicate, clear notes filled the air like drops of refreshing rain, enhancing the beauty of this ancient baroque building. Tears welled up.

I sniffed and waited for the finish before leaning over to my new gentlemen friend and whispering, "I forgot my tissue." He reached into the inside pocket of his suitcoat for his handkerchief and offered it to me with a smile.

"No paper?"

He grinned, shook his head, and motioned for me to accept it.

"Tsk. I'm sorry. Thank you so much."

He smiled bigger.

Tenor Mattia Nebbiai, took the stage, also in a smart tuxedo, and sang Puccini's Tosca, Vissi d'arte. His voice and presence were incredible throughout the performance.

Soprano Clara Polito, in a full length black dress with a soft pink scarf at her neck, entered, bowed and approached the piano, nodding for the music to begin. She sang three pieces, including V. Bellini's Norma, Casta Diva. Her voice was strong, her enunciation immaculate, bereft of tension.

I was transformed.

At the end, my neighbor and I were applauding in sync. We stood and continued clapping until the artists left the stage for the last time.

"Wasn't that spectacular," he said reaching to shake my hand, "I'm Bernard."

"Completely breathtaking. I teared up at the first note. Thank you so much for you your handkerchief. I'll wash it and get it back to you, I promise. I'm Diann."

Bernard, probably 6 foot 8 inches tall, was an attorney from Leeds, England. He would be in Lucca for four nights.

"Would you like to join me for a glass of wine?" he asked.

We retreated to the nearest bar for rossa vino and talked music, Europe, and travel. We laughed and sneered about the crazy 2016 U.S. presidential election and Brexit.

Four hours later, we agreed to meet the next afternoon to walk around the beautiful walls of Lucca.

I was comforted, knowing it would be lovely to have an interesting companion for change.

CHAPTER FIVE

Banking, Debit Cards and Frequent Flyer Credit Cards

Introduction

This Chapter provides simple but important information about taking care of your finances through your bank and smart options for taking advantage of credit cards usage while traveling.

Banking and Debit Cards

Banking fees have doubled and tripled since the Wall Street debacle in 2007. And, and many times, I didn't even know fees were added, unless I looked closely at my statement. The fees silently creeped in.

When Bank of America began charging me, "nickel and diming" me for every little service, I was not happy. Finally, they made an incredible error. I deposited a very large amount of money into my savings account. When I went home to review my account online, I saw that they had mistakenly recorded it as a withdrawal!

Now, come on. This level of ripping me off with stupid service fees and this incredible error were beyond beyond! Needless to say, I gave them MORE than "what for." Their response was less than satisfactory to me. Actually, they seemed to brush it off as a simple error, easily corrected.

I closed my accounts and began my search for a reasonable and competent institution.

I found Charles Schwab worked best for my needs. First, Schwab has NO fees…none! I pay my all my bills online through their bill pay service. I receive my income by direct deposit. As a result, I just go to one place to go to check on my finances and pay bills. And, of course, I get a free debit card.

This card is perfect for traveling everywhere. There are no foreign transactions fees and no ATM fees. The debit card works everywhere, at all ATM's throughout the world. And, although I might have to pay ATM fees at the time I withdraw cash, Schwab automatically reimburses me for any and all ATM fees at the end of the month. This applies to both foreign and domestic ATMs, too.

I'm not suggesting that you go to Schwab. I'm simply sharing my experiences. I have talked with others and found they many people are happy to pay fees if they get exceptional service. So, again, as I have said throughout this Guide, do what suits your needs.

Especially with regard to the best service for travel, I encourage you to check your interests and priorities with the benefits offered by your bank, credit cards, and debit cards.

Note, I only use my debit card at the ATM machine. And, I used my credit cards for all purchases, online and at the markets, grocery, restaurants, etc. I also pay off the balance at the end of the month.

(A special note regarding debit cards. I encourage you to avoid using your debit card to purchase airline tickets. Even if your debit card has a Visa or MasterCard logo, if the airline cancels your flight or goes out of business, you cannot expect the same protections you enjoy with a Visa or MasterCard credit account. With a credit card, you can request a chargeback in the amount of your ticket within 60 days of your purchase.)

Frequent Flyer/Point Credit Cards

Of course, using a credit card abroad is ideal for all sorts of reasons.

For example, you can avoid carrying lots of cash. You can keep track of your purchases.

And, unlike in the United States, transactions take place right there in your presence. Even at restaurants, rather than waiters taking your card to a back room, out of your sight and performing the transaction, the waiters bring a portable machine to your table. Your credit card never leaves your sight. This obviously cuts down on potential identity theft or someone accessing your credit card information.

I suggest you consider credit cards that also earn points for flights, accommodation and other rewards.

Frequent flyer credit cards offer points for every $1 spent, which you can then redeem flights, upgrades and other rewards. You can also enjoy a range of additional features including complimentary travel insurance (See Chapter Three), bonus point offers, airline lounge access, promotional interest rates, etc.

I carry an American Express Delta card, a Master card for American Airlines, and a Visa card for United Airlines. When I initially registered for these cards, they all had special promotions. That is, they waived the annual fee for the first year and gave two points for each dollar for a limited time. Also, this special offer included an outstanding benefit: if I spent $3,000 in six months, I would be awarded additional points.

I use these cards for all my purchases, from flights to lodging, restaurants, T-Mobile payments, Netflix, Google Plus movies, groceries, clothing…everything! And, of course I pay off the balance every month, never paying interest charges.

What does this do besides give me frequent flyer miles? It helps me keep track of my spending budget and it tracks details I need when income tax time rolls around.

How many cards to take?

I suggest you take at least two credit cards. Heaven forbid you should lose one, you always have a second. I have three because not all places will take American Express; however, I want American Express because of the additional benefits it provides.

Before you leave on your trip, let your credit card companies know where you are going and the length of time you will be away. This will
avoid their security system kicking in and blocking your purchases.

There are so many great choices for credit cards now and great deals pop up all the time as banks continue to try to get our business. I can't list everything in this guide book and even if I did, the information would be outdated before it went to press.

Therefore, I suggest you access a website to compare frequent flyer credit cards and learn more about them, including how these cards work, tips for earning and using points, features to compare when you're looking at frequent flyer credit cards and insights to help you choose the right card for you. One such site is Finder.com.au. You may know of others, of course. However, you may to begin with Finder.
www.finder.com.au/credit-cards/frequent-flyer-credit-cards

CHAPTER SIX

Communication

Introduction
Cell Phone Options
      Register your phone for an international/global plan
          with your current carrier.
    Bring your own phone and do everything over WIFI.
    Buy a SIM card in your destination country.
Other Ways to Communicate
Battery Pack
Keeping up with U.S. News

Introduction

Are you wondering how to stay connected with friends and family back home? The number of easy and even free options might surprise you.

Having a mobile device, such as laptop, notepad, notebook, and a cell phone, can help you make the most of your travel time, and not just for communicating.

There are all sorts of useful and free technology available to you, from maps/GPS when finding your way walking or driving, enhanced sightseeing with audio tours and podcasts, calls to restaurants for reservations while riding the bus, or buying advanced tickets for performances and museums…and have them sent right to your phone. I focus on Apps for your phone in the next Chapter, but, for now, let's look at cell phone options, other ways to communicate, and the essential battery pack.

Cell Phone Options

You simply must take a phone. While I seldom use my phone to make local calls while traveling abroad, I frequently use my free apps to make free calls to the United States as well as to my new friends all over the world.

To stay connected, here are three basic phone options.

1. Register your phone for an international/global plan with your current carrier. For those of you who don't travel as frequently or for as long as I do, it's easiest to set up your own mobile phone with a basic international calling and/or data plan that's customized to your needs — and it doesn't have to cost an arm and a leg.

Check to see if your carrier has a global calling plan that cuts the per-minute cost of phone calls and a flat-fee data plan that includes a certain amount of megabytes. Your normal plan may already include international coverage, as T-Mobile does.

- <u>Confirm that your phone will work abroad.</u> Nearly all newer phones work fine abroad (as do older phones purchased through AT&T and T-Mobile), but it's smart to check with your carrier if you're unsure.
- <u>Research your provider's international rates.</u> Plan pricing varies by carrier. Call your provider or check their website for the latest pricing.

You get to travel with all of your contact information and your U.S. phone number, making it easy to connect with folks back home. With the cost of international plans dropping, more and more travelers are willing to pay for the freedom to call, text, and go online anytime, anywhere.

Roaming with your own phone outside the U.S. generally comes with extra charges, categorized in three services: (1) making voice calls, (2) sending texts, or (3) accessing data (going online over a cellular network rather than WIFI, also called "data roaming."

If you plan to bring your own phone, decide how you will use it. You may choose to use it minimally, for example, and decide to avoid texting. You need to decide how often you will use it to go online and check your email or access websites, or using phone apps that require WIFI, etc. Talk with your carrier about this to determine the best plan to purchase given your planned use of data.

- Activate international service. A day or two before you leave, log on to your mobile phone account or call your provider to activate international roaming for voice, text, and/or data (whichever features you plan to use), and sign up for any international plans.

- Be sure cancel international service when you get home. When you return from your vacation, cancel any add-on plans that you activated for your trip. (You may forget this and/or be too involved in trying to re-enter your previous life and forget. To be safe, mark this task on your calendar and create a reminder.)

2. Bring your own phone and do everything over WIFI. More budget-conscious travelers can forego their carrier's international plans altogether and do everything over WIFI. Not only can you use WIFI to get online, but you can also make phone calls and send text messages at no charge. Remember, in this case you need to find a hotspot. Hotspots are available everywhere, usually in bars, cafes, and restaurants. However, courtesy dictates that you sit down and order at least a cup of coffee.

3. Buy a SIM card in your destination country. This option works best for people who plan to call often while traveling. Of course, you can buy a SIM card, which is useable in a variety of countries. A SIM card is a microchip that stores your phone number and other data. You take out your SIM card and replace it with this new SIM card, or into a cheap mobile phone that you buy for your trip. This gives you a number in your destination country and at the same rates locals enjoy.

Please note, SIM cards are not accessible on some phones. This is the case with my iPhone 6+ Apple phone.

Before I began traveling, I switched to T-Mobile. When I switched, T-Mobile paid the penalty for cancelling my contract with my other carrier. With T-Mobile, I have free international data and text messaging in over 140 countries. That means free roaming which generally allows me to access the internet at all times. (I say "generally" because sometimes, in the mountains, on trains and planes, and on the bus in tunnels, internet is simply not available.) And, all calls while in those 140 plus countries are a mere 20 cents a minute. Video calls can zap your data, but not with free roaming. I pay $80 a month for excellent coverage and service.

Other Ways to Communicate

Apple FaceTime Video - You can use FaceTime video to connect with anyone over WIFI, as long as both parties have a Mac, iPhone, or iPad. The software is pretty simple to use and standard with all Apple devices that feature a camera. If you're doing it over data, keep it short: Video calls quickly drain a data plan.

Facebook Messaging — If you don't have a Facebook page, create one and register for Facebook messaging. It's free, easy, and has a visual option.

Pocket WIFI - If you are worried about keeping connected while traveling, make sure to purchase a mobile hotspot before your trip. I have read about a new device called the Teppy. It's available in many different countries and allows you to rent a wireless hotspot for around $9 a day. Frequent travelers may opt to purchase a device for $99 and pay $8 a day. Check for more information:
www.tepwireless.com/WIFI/global

Skype Video - One of the simplest ways to stay connected abroad is Skype. Skype works on almost every internet-connected device. You can also buy Skype credit and make phone calls on your phone or on your computer to landlines and mobile phones.

WhatsApp and Viber – These apps for your phone are very easy to use. When you call using these apps, the recipient needs to have the app as well. Set up your contacts before you go on your trip.

Battery Pack

When we talk about phones and how to use them when traveling, it is imperative we also discuss how to ensure that your phone and all your information is always accessible.

When I first started traveling, I used my phone constantly and I ran my battery down. This always seemed to happen when I needed stored information the most! For example, at the airline ticket counter, or trying to tell the Uber driver my destination. Or, and this happened to me in Lisbon over and over again as I walked around the city, using my HERE GPS App to guide me to and from my destinations. GPS Apps simply drain batteries. And there I was, in unfamiliar surroundings, out of juice!

Finally, I bought a battery pack and it has been a life saver. It's charged all the time and always in my purse or backpack (along with the phone cord), just in case I decide to be spontaneous and take a detour. No worries about being adrift without my phone and GPS to find my way home. Just plug in and continue to enjoy myself.

You can get them at technology store and online. They range from $20 to $50. I have a Lumina. I bought it from Amazon for $19.99.

If you decide to buy one, be sure it's high quality and has fast charging capabilities. You will not be sorry!

Keeping up with U.S. News

Frankly, I am riveted to the news back home. I am either on my phone or my laptop sometime during the day every day to catch up on severe weather, the Sunday morning programs, world affairs, sports, and yes, I'll admit it: politics.

If I were traveling for a short amount of time, these topics could wait. I could catch up when I return. But, I'm always traveling and, as a result, I need to have a way to remain current. Many of the

hotels and apartments I have stayed in have television. Fewer, however, have programs in English. For those areas of the world that do have television programming in English, it usually is the BBC (British Broadcasting Corporation) or CNN. Yet it is often only for an hour or so during the morning hours. And, besides the obvious narrow perspective, it isn't timely, given the different time zones.

What do I do?

I have gravitated to accessing the news on my laptop. I live-stream CBNews Live. It's available 24 hours a day and it's free. I also find "news" a day after it is broadcasted by googling YOUTUBE channels.

Finally, HULU is also a relatively inexpensive (less than $40/month) avenue to accessing news, sports, and more. While HULU is only available in the United States, you can "play" with your "online location" by using a VPN (Virtual Private Network). That is to say, you can trick HULU into thinking you are in the United States by streaming via your VPN in a U.S. location.

(Please forward to the next Chapter to read more specifically about the VPN details.)

Vignette: Barga, Italy

What a treat! Barga, located in the Sechio Valley, is a calm, peaceful community, full of alluring sights, scenes and very pleasant locals. A simple forty-minute train ride from Lucca to this sweet little, virtually untouched, city of 10,000 residents; then a leisurely hour walk, four kilometers, up the hill to Barga proper, past impressive private homes, all behind ornate walls and fences.

Nearly every gate was adorned with a sign saying "beware of the dog," but, happily, only one proud pooch approached from behind his gate to protest our presence. Bernard and I, undeterred, pressed onward and upwards.

Bernard, my British friend who I had met a few days previous at a Puccini Opera performance in Lucca, was the impeccable companion. He took care of all the niggling details: the train, the tickets, the trek, the restaurant, and especially, the fine wine. As for me and my responsibilities, I simply enjoyed myself, snapping incredible photos all along the way.

First, a brief history about Barga.

Barga lies 35 kilometers (22 miles) north of the provincial capital, Lucca. It is overlooked by the village of Albiano, a località of Barga, which in the 10th century was the site of a castle protecting the town. Pania della Croce, a mountain of the Apuan Alps, dominates the surrounding chestnut trees, grape vines and olive grove, is a magnificent backdrop for this ancient community, named "The most Scottish town in Italy," reminiscent of Scotland.

In the 9th century, Barga is mentioned as a family feud of the Lombard family of Rolanding. Later, in the 11th century, Barga was obtained from Matilda of Tuscany. She was one of the few medieval women to be remembered for her military accomplishments, which allowed her to dominate all the territories north of the Church State. She founded one hundred churches.

Today, the Collegiate Church of San Cristoforo is Barga's greatest attraction. Built during the 11th to the 16th centuries, it is the main example of Romanesque architecture in the Serchio Valley. Of the original church, built in local limestone, only parts of the façade remain.

The interior has a nave and two aisles. It houses a large (3.5 m) wooden statue of St. Christopher, patron of the city. The pulpit (built in the 12th century) was designed by Guido Bigarelli da Como, and has four red marble columns resting on lion sculptures. The campanile, or bell tower, contains three bells, the oldest of which dates to the 16th century.

When Matilda died, she left all her properties, including the Serchio Valley, to the Church. Unfortunately, leaving all properties to the Church was not a very a popular decision and caused a war. As a result of the war, the diocese of Lucca was abolished and split between several parties, including Pisa. Barga took advantage of this relationship with Pisa, became allies, and in the 13th century, together fought Lucca. Finally, in 1236, Barga was subordinated to Lucca.

Later, Barga became an important trade city. The city developed as a castle surrounded by a line of walls. Through all of this history of changing hands and wars, two gates (Porta Reale and Porta Macchiaia) managed to survive.

The town was well known during the Middle Ages for the manufacture of silk threads which were exported to major centers such as Florence. In the Middle Ages, Lucca and Pisa battled frequently to conquer the wealthy town and the surrounding territory, and for a time, Barga was part of the Florentine dominion, and later, a part of the Duchy and Grand Duchy of Tuscany. Barga has been a part of the province of Lucca since 1923.

The region was part of the Gothic Line in World War II, and was the scene of fierce fighting between the Allies and Germans from October 1944 until April, 1945.

This is the history that Bernard and I decided to explore. What a treat! We came upon a series of sweet surprises...including a red telephone booth transformed into free library, yellow and orange hibiscus, roses bursting coral and red, and charming shops.

We stopped for lunch at Ristorante Capretz, on Piazza Salvo Salvi, at the top of the city. The Chianti was perfect complement to roasted vegetables and luscious veal steak. The view was breathtaking through the potted herbs and brilliant red, yellow and orange flowers perched on the rod iron railing, framing the colorful town below, completely surrounded by magnificent blue-green mountains.

We were in Barga for just over four hours and, therefore unable to take advantage of the Opera and Jazz festivals, or even the weekly Friday night Jazz. Bummer!

Timing is everything, isn't it?

A quick bus ride allowed us to skip the hour walk down to the train back to Lucca. Incidentally, the Barga train station office was closed and the ticket machine was out of order. That didn't stop us from boarding, of course. We expected a conductor to collect our money for the return. But, alas, no. No conductor, at all!

The dreamy free ride back to Lucca was a perfect ending to a lovely day.

I encourage you to slip away to Barga whenever you are near Lucca, Pisa, or Cinque Terra. It's a breath of fresh air and a well-deserved break from all those pesky tourists.

CHAPTER SEVEN

Travel Apps

Introduction
Essential Apps
Useful Apps
Nice-to-Have Apps

Introduction

Frankly, I just don't know how we traveled before the invention of the app. Yes, I traveled without apps years ago. Of course, I was unaware of this wonderful new technology. Ignorance is bliss, you know, and we all managed. But, no more!

Apps confessions: I cannot live comfortably without my apps! More important, why should I?

Below, I have listed all the apps I use from the Essential, to Useful, and finally Nice-to-Have. Take your pick, but I encourage you to add the "Essential" apps to your phone. Some of them already come with your cell phone.

Most are free. Those that are not free are worth every penny for ease of travel, including quick access to important information for both convenience and safety; organizing your personal information, as well as transportation and lodging reservations.

Note, most Apps require WIFI in order to work. Please look for that information among the list below.

Essential Apps

Can I Eat This? App: Montezuma's revenge, Delhi belly, or travelers' diarrhea—whatever you call it, it can ruin your international trip. Help prevent travelers' diarrhea by using Centers for Disease Control and Prevention's (CDC) Can I Eat This? App. Select the country you're in and answer a few simple questions about what you're thinking about eating or drinking, and Can I Eat This? Will tell you whether it's likely to be safe. You can be confident that your food and drink choices won't make you spend your international trip in the bathroom. Key features: authoritative recommendations from the CDC and you can access recommendations offline (no data connection needed).

Clock/alarm/time/zones: My phone came with the "clock" app. Check the apps on your phone. You probably have a similar app. When you are traveling through time zones, it's very easy to get confused. Besides, your biological clock gets all screwed up when your sleep habits are interrupted. It is great to know the time in your current location, of course; however, it is also good to know the current time back home to avoid calling your children in the middle of the night.

Program your app to include cities that are important to you so just with a click you can know the difference in hours. Finally, an alarm is very important, especially if you aren't totally confident that the hotel wake-up call will actually occur.

Currency exchange: I have the XE app, but, of course, any app will do, if the currency rates on the app are based on live mid-market rates. I use this app frequently to check prices on flights and hotels, and also when shopping. It's also extremely useful when exchanging money at a bank or other service location. I compare their rate with the live mid-rate to see how much the exchange fee actually is. If it's too high, I first try to negotiate. If we don't reach agreement, I kindly excuse myself and go elsewhere.

FindMyiPhone App typically is already on your iPhone. This app lets you easily track down a lost device or, failing that, remotely lock or wipe it so that it can't easily be accessed. All you need to do is make sure that you turn it on before you lose your device. Make sure you understand how to use it before you leave home.

FindMyPhone App is Google's native find your phone app. The app lets you ring your phone, wipe and even show a message. The app is excellent because you can make a good attempt to find your phone, in case it's in the sofa or under the bed. Worse case, you can wipe it if you can't find it. It's free. Be sure you load this app before you leave for your adventure and, of course, make sure you know what to do.

GPS: I use the HERE App, but again, any app will do. Many people use GoogleMaps app. Both are free. Go online and download the maps, regions and/or countries. Then, you can access those maps at any time, even when you are off line. Remember, no downloads, no off-line access.

The off-line access is the key to using the app. I use it when I walk and when I drive. It especially comes in handy when taking a taxi.

Did you ever experience a taxi driver who would take you all around the city just to drop you off a few blocks from your departure location? What a rip off! And, how could you even know if you were being ripped off until after the fact? Ah, but the GPS app changes all that.

Now, when I enter the taxi, I automatically show the driver the address of the destination on my GPS app. It will be in the language of the country, of course. I don't have to try to say the destination in Turkish, for example. The driver can read it and confirm he/she is familiar with the address. Furthermore, the driver sees I have a GPS app and is aware that I know exactly where we are and the route to the destination. Potential rips offs are eliminated, especially when my GPS App voice says aloud, "turn right at ….."

TravelSmart (Allianz Global Assist): The perfect extension of your travel insurance policy. But you don't have to buy an Allianz insurance plan to use the app. What I especially like about this app is the international hospital search which allows me to locate the closest pre-screened medical facility with a geo-aware hospital search. It includes what numbers to dial no matter which country I am in. It provides current location information to reach local police, an ambulance, or the fire department. And, you can find the right medication anywhere in the world with a medication dictionary, and also translate first aid terms into multiple languages.

(Note, I am not promoting Allianz! I happen to have this App because I did, at one time, purchase insurance from this company. I kept it because it's very useful even without the policy. When and if you decide to purchase insurance, check to see if the agency has such an app so that you have immediate access to the insurance company should to need help, or need to file a claim.)

TravWell App: Plan safe and healthy international travel. Build a trip to get destination-specific immunization recommendations, a checklist of what you need to do to prepare for travel, and a customizable healthy travel packing list. The app also lets you store travel documents, keep a record of your medications and immunizations, and set reminders to get vaccine booster doses or take medicines while you're traveling. Key features include: Authoritative recommendations from the Centers for Disease Control and Prevention, during-travel features available offline (no data connection needed), fully customizable to do list and packing list, and emergency services phone numbers for every destination.

TripIt: Get a master itinerary for every trip with all your travel plans in one place. With this app, your itinerary is as close as your mobile device (smartphone, tablet, computer, or wearable. Also is iOS and Android and you can access your itinerary offline. View your confirmation number on the way to the airport. Get directions to your hotel when you land. It's like having a personal assistant who's one step ahead.

This app is a life saver and a money saver. For me, it's hard to keep track with all those email confirmations coming in. Then, I am notorious for my inability to find the confirmation email when I need it, especially since I need to be online to access email and often WIFI connection is challenged.

The solution is TripIt. TripIt alerts me to check-in times, upcoming flights and lodging reservations. It even alerted me when I hadn't reserved lodging in Cusco, Peru. Well, I had, but I had failed to forward the confirmation email to my TripIt App! It's simple and it's free.

VPN: Virtual Private Network App. What is a VPN? Few people actually know. Most important, a VPN secures both your computer's internet connection and your cell phone's internet connection to guarantee that all of the data you're sending and receiving are encrypted and secured from prying eyes.

You really should be using a VPN, and even if you don't think so now, at some point in the future you may consider it JU.S.T as important as your internet connection.

VPN's are useful for many reasons, however, for our purposes I will limit this discussion to (1) the privacy minded and security advocate, (2) the sport enthusiast traveler, and (3) the frugal traveler who is looking for all options to find less expensive flights.

The privacy minded and security advocate: Whether in a strictly monitored environment or a completely free and open one, this person uses VPN services to keep communications secure and encrypted and away from prying eyes, whether at home or abroad. To this person, unsecured connections mean someone is reading what they say. And, this is indeed possible while traveling, especially when banking, purchasing and paying bills online, and checking on credit cards purchases and payments. My VPN is always engaged in these cases. Users need to sure the VPN is active when posting any vital information, i.e., passport number, social security number, credit card numbers, bank account numbers, etc.

The sports enthusiast traveler: People in this category want to watch the Olympics live, as they happen, without dealing with their crummy local networks. They want to watch their favorite TV shows live rather than waiting to view it later use a new web service or application that looks great but for some reason is limited to a specific country or region and/or restricted in certain countries. A VPN can circumscribe all of that by using the streaming feature.

For example, HULU is limited to the United States. That is, you cannot buy a membership unless you are in the U.S....or unless you make HULU THINK you are in the U.S. but activating your VPN and stream it to an U.S. location, such as Phoenix, Seattle or San Francisco. *Viola!*

The frugal traveler who is looking for all options to find less expensive flights: As discussed in Chapter One, a VPN is handy when searching and comparing flights. It allows you to play with your "online location."

For example, even though you may be in New York this morning, seeing flight prices in dollars, you could turn your VPN on to the UK and be quoted prices in British pounds. For many flights this won't make much difference, but for some you'll actually find real savings for booking in one currency versus another. Norwegian Airlines and flights within Asia are prime examples.

As for me, I always have my Baron VPN active when I'm at the airport or train station...even in restaurants. I don't understand everything I know about identify theft, except that it is rampant and the creeps find way to hack into accounts despite more and more technological and fancy efforts to stop them.

To purchase or not to purchase! If you plan to travel for any length of time, check your bank balance, make any online purchases that require your inserting your credit card number, or doing anything online that requires you to post vital information, you simply must have a VPN for your own protection.

Fees vary according to level of service. I pay $70/year and have my VPN both on my phone and my computer. Whatever you do, don't try to get away with a free VPN. It's a scam!

Besides Baron, here are some highly recommended VPN providers: proXPM, TorVPN, TorGuard, and WiTopia.

One final note, VPN's interfere with my Netflix account. I have to disable my Baron VPN to watch Netflix. But, seriously, it is not a problem. I just don't do online banking at the same time.

WhatsApp, Viber, Skype and Facebook Messenger: Free online cell phone calling service, with the video. You can talk and see each other at the same time. Think about how much money these apps save! Note, in order to call on these apps, you can only call those who have also have the app. Take care of that before you leave on your trip. Although, it is possible to manage it after you leave and meet new friends, as well. (See CHAPTER SIX: Communication.)

Useful Apps

Exercise Apps: There is an app for everything! Here is list of five exercise apps: MapMyRun, MyFitnessPal, Nike Training Club, Pocket Yoga, and Sworkit. All of these apps focus on forms of exercise that meet everyone's need, no matter if you are a crazed athletic or a couch potato. Most also include some aspect of diet. Take your pick to stay in shape and feeling good throughout your travels. See page 37 for the details about each app.

MobilePass: This app is designed to allow you to breeze through customs when returning to the United States. After a long flight back to the U.S., bypass those long lines at immigration and customs!

Enter your profile information as it appears on your valid, official passport. You can set up profiles for your entire family. Your information will be encrypted and shared only with U.S. Customs and Border Patrol (CBP). Answer CBP's four brief questions about your trip. Once you are at your port of entry (airport or sea port), connect to wireless or WIFI and submit your data to CBP. Within a few seconds, you will receive a CBP receipt with an encrypted barcode. Your receipt will be valid for four hours. Follow the Mobile Passport Control signs to the designated Mobile Passport Control line. Show your passport to the CBP officer and scan the barcode on the CBP receipt. And that's it!

Note: this service is not live at every entry into the U.S.; but, at one cruise port (Port Everglades in Florida) and twenty-four airports, at the time of this writing.

Open Table – This free app lets you find restaurants based on location, popularity, price, and availability. You can read restaurant reviews, see menus, know approximately what a meal will cost and make reservations without phone calls, even when on the run. It includes optional mobile payment integration. Great selection of restaurants and helpful details.

Translator App: Gotta have it for obvious reasons, but, especially for spur of the moment conversations. Plus, it is fun and instructional! It's free and requires WIFI.

- **Uber App**: Taxi service operates in 633 cities worldwide. Uber drivers use their own cars although drivers can rent a car to drive with Uber, providing less expensive service for passengers than the taxi companies and, no money exchanges hands. You load your credit card information when you register. At the time of service, click pay and you are ready to go. I use it everywhere!

Weather channel: Another free app which I use daily! You more than likely already have it on your phone.

Nice-to-Have Apps

I have the following apps on my phone and I use them, but only occasionally, when I need to check something and am away from my laptop.

Duolingo App is a great app for learning language. It's is the best, right up there with Babbel and RosettaStone. And, it's free!

The following apps below are nice to have if you are away from your laptop or a computer, you have internet and you need something fast:

Airbnb
Booking.com
eDreams.com
Renfe Ticket
Momondo
And, any other website service you like and want to have at your fingertips.

Diann Schindler, Ph.D.

Vignette: Cusco, Peru

I trekked, on foot, virtually straight up a paved road to the archaeological site called Sacahuayman, a citadel on the northern outskirts of the city and at the top of the city of Cusco. I walked almost two hours and shot photos along the way, not only because the views were breathtaking, but also because the altitude...11,500 feet above sea level... was breathtaking!

When I finally arrived, I learned that the tour of Sacahuayman took at least five hours for a fee of 70 euros. To be perfectly honest, I just didn't want to spend the time or the money. I took another option: to ride on horseback for about three hours for fifty euros and visit an area very near Sacahuayman.

A taxi driver took me to an old barn, tucked away on the side of the mountain. Tired horses, saddled with leather and thick wool, stood in black mud, heads hanging low in rest.

Yeah, on horseback to the top of Cusco!

There were three of us who would be led by a Peruvian girl named Sandy...although, I doubt if that was truly her name. As we mounted, our horses perked up, eager to get moving. One of the horses had a lively foal that scampered along with us.

Sandy walked along on foot, through the mud with her purple, pokadot canvas flats. She spoke no English, nor did she understand English. In fact, I was the only one who spoke English. Gladly, I was forced to dig deep for Spanish I just knew had to be in my brain somewhere.

We climbed steep inclines through stones, water, fallen tree limbs and twisted around boulders and trees. Our horses were well trained and never once stopped to eat. Rather, they obeyed Sandy as she urged them with her special click sounds and faint whistles. The horses and the foal consistently forged forward over the treacherous terrain, cooled by the mountain air and the shadows of the chachacomo and elderberry trees.

After about an hour, the trail opened up to the warm sun, peaceful green pastures with yellow wild flowers, and the stone ruins of ancient architecture, including a

fortress and a sacred temple. We saw
hectares of wheat-like foliage that served
of city of Cusco in the distance below
higher, and explored while our horses
spring, sweet grass in an open field. T

Thirty glorious minutes later, we
something to me in Spanish and I
nodded. She led two of my fellow
behind some trees, out of sight.

I held on for dear li
over again!

I waited there, by myself still in the saddle. As the time passed, I decided to
my phone to video these few moments. The video turned ridiculous because I was
trying to talk to my house. Of course, he ignores me completely, at first. Finally,
my efforts were rewarded. Or so I thought.

Yes, he lifted his head and started moving his body. I just knew he wanted to
talk to me now! I thought he was saying "hello" to me...but not!

(You can find the video on my website DiannAbroad blog entitled "Vamonos,'
Cusco on Horseback."

If you listen carefully at the very end of the video, you can hear a single horse
approaching, galloping and Sandy shouting something in Spanish. I stopped the
video and as quickly as I could, I stored my phone safely in my pocket.

"Vamonos! Vamonos!" Sandy screamed. She was flying in the saddle with no
intentions of slowing down!

My steed whinnied and bounced. He wanted to go! And, so, we did!

We galloped and galloped, and cantered, and, thank goodness, galloped again.
(Cantering is so hard on the ass!) My camera and purse were safe, but bounced
violently, up, down, and around.

I think we galloped for about six or seven minutes, which is actually a long time,
for those of us who haven't even been on a horse in thirty-five years.

e and laughed so hard my nose ran! Man, I'd love to do it all

CHAPTER EIGHT

Safety

Introduction
United States Department of State Travel Alerts: Worldwide Caution
United States Department of State STEP Program
Keep Documents Safe and Accessible
Cell Phone Safety Tips
Personal Safety
      Guidelines

Introduction

Most people, all over the world, are good. Yet, we all know there are plenty of thieves and creeps. I encourage you not to be afraid. Safety is always an issue and the best way to be safe is to be well informed and follow safety guidelines. Rather, I encourage you to be aware, alert and armed with safety practices, outlined in this Chapter.

United States Department of State Travel Alerts: Worldwide Caution

The United States Department of State is key to our safety. It has its pulse on what is happening everywhere, far more than we know. The Department keeps us informed, up to date and connected to the U.S. and to family and friends, at all times, and especially in the case of an emergency.

Consular officers around the world compile country-specific information, travel alerts, travel warnings, fact sheets and emergency messages to provide you with timely and accurate information about every country where you may travel.

The Department includes reports on risks and security threats so that you can make informed decisions about your travel plans and activities.

The Department of State is continually providing U.S. citizens traveling abroad, with information about safety and security events. The Department updates the Worldwide Caution reports with information on the continuing threat of terrorist actions, political violence, and criminal activity against U.S. citizens and interests abroad as often as it deems necessary to keep us armed with pertinent information for your safety.

As terrorist attacks, political upheaval, and violence often take place without any warning, the Department strongly encourages travelers to maintain a high level of vigilance and take appropriate steps to increase our security awareness when traveling. To better prepare for possible emergencies, we are encouraged to read Country Specific Information pages, Travel Warnings, and Travel Alerts on travel.state.gov before planning a trip.

The Department uses these security messages to convey information about terrorist threats, security incidents, planned demonstrations, natural disasters, etc.

In an emergency, please contact the nearest U.S. Embassy or Consulate or call the following numbers: 1-888-407-4747 (toll-free in the United States and Canada) or 1-202-501-4444 from other countries.

At the time of this writing, U.S. government facilities worldwide remain in a heightened state of alert. These facilities may temporarily close or periodically suspend public services to assess their security posture. In those instances, U.S. embassies and consulates will make every effort to provide emergency services to U.S. citizens. U.S.

citizens abroad are urged to monitor the local news and maintain contact with the nearest U.S. embassy or consulate.

Terrorist groups including ISIS, al-Qa'ida, their associates, and those inspired by such organizations, are intent on attacking U.S. citizens wherever they are. Extremists may use conventional or non-conventional weapons to target U.S. government and private interests. Terrorists are increasingly using less sophisticated methods of attack to more effectively target crowds, including the use of edged weapons, pistols, and vehicles as weapons. Extremists increasingly aim to assault "soft" targets, such as:

- high-profile public events (sporting contests, political rallies, demonstrations, holiday events, celebratory gatherings, etc.)
- hotels, clubs, and restaurants
- places of worship
- schools
- parks
- shopping malls and markets
- tourism infrastructure
- public transportation systems
- airports

In multiple regions, terrorists, guerrilla groups, and criminals seek to kidnap U.S. citizens to finance their operations or for political purposes. The Department also remains concerned that terrorists could again seek to down aircraft using concealed explosives or hijack commercial flights.

Do not travel to any country to participate in armed conflict. You are reminded that fighting on behalf of or providing other forms of support to designated terrorist organizations can constitute the provision of material support for terrorism, which is a serious crime that can result in penalties, including prison time and large fines.

In addition to concerns stemming from terrorism, travelers should be alert to the possibility of political unrest, violence, demonstrations, and criminal activities when traveling. Country-specific information pages and Travel Warnings should be consulted to obtain the latest data on such threats.

For further information: See the Department of State's travel website for the Worldwide Caution, Travel Warnings, Travel Alerts, and Country Specific Information. www.travel.state.gov

United States Department of State STEP Program

Enroll in the Department's Smart Traveler Enrollment Program (STEP) to receive security messages and make it easier to locate you in an emergency. The Smart Traveler Enrollment Program (STEP) is a free service that allows U.S. citizens traveling or living abroad to enroll with the nearest U.S. embassy or consulate. Enrollment is free, of course, and provides you, through email, the following:

• The latest and most up-to-date safety and security information for your destination country, helping you make informed decisions about your travel plans.

• The U.S. Embassy in your travel destination country will contact you in an emergency, whether natural disaster, civil unrest, or family emergency.

• The U.S. Department of State will help your family and friends get in touch with you in an emergency.

Just sign up once, and then add trips later for all your future travel plans. www.travel.state.gov/content/passports/en/go/step.html

Keep Documents Safe and Accessible

How do you keep track of all your important documents when you travel without having to carrying stacks of important papers? And, how can you have easy access to each document in case of an emergency?

Here is a simple plan. Yes, it require preliminary work; however, when the work is complete, you can feel confident that everything of superior importance is in order, safe, and accessible. It's good to know, if something unfortunate should occur, you are ready to handle it. This is like your very own personal insurance plan.

1. What are "important documents?" Here is a list.

✓ Vital Records: Driver's license, international driver's license, passport, and visas
✓ Insurance Policies: auto, life, health, and travel insurance. Have at least the policy number and insurance company contact information for each type of coverage.
✓ Medical Information: Immunization and other medical records, prescription information (drug name and dosage), health insurance identification cards, and, if under a doctor's care, include physician names and phone numbers.
✓ Banking and credit/debit cards: Bank name and account numbers and credit/debit card numbers

2. Scan copies of all your important documents and e-mail to yourself.

3. Store in the Cloud through Google Drive or send to a Dropbox folder, just in case you lose your phone. If you need to print them while you are abroad, go to the business office at your hotel or to an internet café.

I needed to print out some documents when I was in Marseilles, France. I was in an Airbnb without a printer, of course. I was in a rush and was not successful at finding an internet café quickly. I stopped into a very fine hotel just steps away from the Old Port and asked to use their business office. I explained that I was not a guest and was happy to pay for the cost of printing. They were very gracious and insisted on printing my documents at the front desk and at no charge. Viola!

---

4. Store everything in one app. This brings me back to the TripIt App, explained briefly in previous Chapter. Let's go deeper.

The TripIt app has "Traveler Profile" feature that is digital place to store scanned versions of everything! Information is available both on the app on your phone, as well as through its website.

The information is also stored offline so you can access it even when you don't have a data connection.

TripIt says that your profile can store "almost any document," but it comes with 20 preset document and contact types to help you get started. You add everything right on your phone and access it with just a few taps later. All your sensitive data is protected behind a four-digit PIN, so if you happen to lose your phone you don't have to worry about your info ending up in nefarious hands.

Meanwhile, remember Step 3, above. Should you lose your phone, not all is lost, because you previously stored everything in Cloud or to a Dropbox folder.

Using TripIt is a lot safer than storing things on your phone's camera roll, and can make filling out forms at the airport or pulling up your doctor's phone number in an emergency a lot easier. If you do end up in a situation where you lose your phone or luggage, there's also definitely something to be said for having all that information available via the web.

TripIt and the Traveler Profile feature is free to use, but the $49/year Pro version of the app offers additional features like seat tracking, refund notifications, and real-time flight alerts.

Note, TripIt is the app I use. I receive no benefits from TripIt. I read about it before I began my worldwide adventures. It has worked for me and my experience makes it is easy for me to describe. I'm positive there are other just-as-good-as TripIt apps available. The point is, such an app is essential for organized and safe travel.

Follow these four steps prior to your departure and you are free to enjoy your trip without worrying about important documents.

Cell Phone Safety Tips

What would I do without my cell phone? I have everything on my phone. I mean, everything! But, you know, thousands of cell phones are stolen each year. Phones are a valuable item and thieves know that. Phones can be easy to steal and easy for thieves to sell for a nice profit.

Here are some ways to keep your phone safe and preventative measures to keep your data from getting lost or in the hands of others.

Be aware of your surroundings. When you decide to use your phone, no matter where you are, look around. Make sure you're in a safe place with a bit of protection. Avoid phone use at bus stops, busy street corners, or while walking. Someone could grab your phone on the run while you are still wondering what happened. Find a corner where you can huddle. Better, however, if you're in a busy area or a place you think might be risky, don't use your phone. Wait until you are in a safe place.

Be alert, always. Do you do the tourist walk? That is, are you walking around, looking up at the incredible architecture, with headphones or earbuds, listening to music? Do you focus on your phone apps, like your GPS, totally engaged and unaware of what's happening around you? Be alert and always be aware of your environment. If you find you can't multitask in this way, stop. Find a secure place, check your GPS and then go on your way.

Store in a secure place. Do not store your phone in your back pocket. Yeah, it looks cool, but it is completely unsafe. Pack your phone away in a zippered pocket and never place it on a table of a restaurant. (See my Bogota, Columbia story in the next few pages.) Always know where your phone is. Don't leave it your hotel room. If you don't think you'll need it for the day and don't want to be interrupted, simply shut it off and store it in a safe pocket where you can monitor it. If you are driving, avoid leaving your phone in plain view on the dashboard or seat, even with the windows shut. It's simply too inviting for thieves.

Lock your phone with an unusual password. Should you lose your phone or if someone does steal it, be sure to have locked your phone with an unusual password and keep it locked when not in use.

FindMyiPhone App typically is already on your iPhone. This app lets you easily track down a lost device or, failing that, remotely lock or wipe it so that it can't easily be accessed. All you need to do is make sure that you turn it on before you lose your device. Make sure you understand how to use it before you leave home.

FindMyPhone is Google's native find your phone app. The app lets you ring your phone, wipe and even show a message. The app is excellent because you can make a good attempt to find your phone, in case it's in the sofa or under the bed. Worse case, you can wipe it if you can't find it. It's free. Be sure you load this app before you leave for your adventure and, of course, make sure you know what to do.

Always keep a copy of your phone's registration number in your purse or wallet, as well as instructions for activating any anti-theft devices you may have installed.

If, as I have suggested, you have important papers stored on your phone, download and copy them online PRIOR to your departure.

Personal Safety

In my experience, as a woman traveling alone in the last twenty plus months and to over thirty countries, including parts of the world known for their less than progressive attitudes towards females, I have only felt threatened three times. Two times St. Petersburg, Florida, when I thought someone was breaking into my Airbnb apartment, I called the police. It ended without incident.

And, then there was the time I was in Bogota, Columbia.

I stopped in a lovely, small restaurant in a nice area of Bogota. The restaurant looked like sweet a French bakery with pristine glass and mirrors and colorful South American décor. It was a Sunday afternoon and the restaurant was vacant, except for two female employees, two women eating at another table, and me. No one spoke English and my Spanish from Spain wasn't working at all in South America.

The furniture was tiny. The table was, perhaps, fourteen inches square. The straight back bright yellow chairs were low to the floor. I ordered by pointing to a sandwich under the glass and sat at a table near the front door.
Three nicely dressed thirty-something men with bright, friendly faces entered. All three sat at my tiny table. We were knee-to-knee. When the waiter asked for their order, I understood that they didn't want to eat.

At that moment, I realized two important points. One, if they didn't want to eat in this restaurant, perhaps, these gentlemen had other plans in mind. And, two, their placement at my table blocked me from an easy exit.

I was calm, but I knew these guys were up to no good. My Apple 6+ cell phone was on my lap, tethered to an external battery in my day back pack. The day back pack was on the floor between my feet.

I ate my sandwich.

The man on my right began talking to me in Spanish. I shrugged my shoulders indicating I didn't understand. Then, he then leaned in and began asking me questions in English. I didn't completely ignore him, but I didn't engage. I kept eating and glanced up at the female employee behind the glass counter. Without speaking, she signaled me to be wary. I nodded as subtly as possible.

I sipped my wine.

This same employee took a place mat and utensils from behind the counter to a table, on my right, in the rear of the restaurant. I could barely see her in my peripheral vision. But, I didn't want to turn toward or even allow my eyes to shift away from the table and my guests, especially the talkative one, on my right.

I sensed her effort to communicate with me with her body language. I looked back at her as she nearly imperceptibly jerked her head, ordering me to come to the table she had just prepared.

I turned my attention back to my table. While the others remained silent, my friend on my right continued his efforts to engage me in conversation.

I took another bite of my sandwich.

Then, I slowly slipped my phone into my day back pack and secured the day back pack over my forearm. With two free hands, I picked up my drink and sandwich. Carefully, I stood up from my chair and with a brief smile and a nod to my new friends who had so graciously joined me at my table, I walked, slowly, to the other table, about five feet away.

At the same time, the employee was returning to the counter. The men got up from their chairs and began screaming at her, throwing their arms up in the air. I couldn't understand their words, but it was clear to me that they were telling her to stay out of their business…their business of stealing money and cell phones. She showed no fear. I think she said that she had done nothing wrong and they should take their business elsewhere. She wasn't aggressive; just firm.

I finished my lunch. My wine was especially good following this incident. As I left, we hugged, smiled and hugged again.

I'd say three scares over all is an excellent record and demonstrates my success at practicing my own safety guidelines which I spell out below. Moreover, besides my practice of being to being acutely aware of my surroundings and relying on my gut instinct or "should-I-even-be-here?" detector, I also always listen to the locals. If they say they wouldn't go somewhere or do something in their own city, then I don't either.

Guidelines

1. Plan ahead. Always plan ahead.

2. Check the internet, especially Rome2Rio (see Chapter One) and Uber to plan your for your transportation, even when you are simply exploring or going out in the city for dinner or entertainment. Know how to get to your location and return before your leave your hotel, hostel or apartment.

3. Always take your phone. And, be sure you can call a local, a taxi, the police, the local "911", etc. (See **TravelSmart** App in Chapter Seven.)

4. Keep the address to your accommodation, both in English and the local language. Take a card from the front desk, if available. Write it on your phone notes and in a notebook, should your run out of battery energy. If you traveling with a group, be sure everyone does the same, in case you are separated.

5. Buy insurance and keep you documents on your phone notes. (See Chapter Three.)

6. Register with Smart Traveler Enrollment Program (STEP) with the U.S. Department of State. Record your travel plans, noting the countries you will be visiting. STEP will notify you via email for any crisis or impending danger. (See Chapter Eight.)

7. Use your GPS App (See Chapter Seven) prior to leaving to become familiar with the route, both to and from. Make sure public transportation and/or taxi service is available. Ask the front desk or your host's questions about specific routes for subway, trams and buses. Maybe the train or bus will take you to Point B, but once at Point B, there won't be any cabs for the rest of your night's journey. In some cases, transportation is not available after a certain hour on some days. I always use my HERE App when using Uber or taxi service. I show the address to the driver. As a result, she or he knows I know the route. (And, this makes it less likely the driver will take the long, more expensive, route.)

8. Don't walk alone at night. If you find yourself walking alone at night, walk slightly behind a couple, as if you are a part of their group.

9. Avoid dark or non-tourist areas at night.

10. Avoid large festivals and sporting events where terrorists may attack. If you do go to such events, don't mingle in the center of the crowd. Hang on the outside and always think of an escape route. If you see something suspicious, leave. If you feel uncomfortable, leave.

11. Of course, don't go off alone with a stranger. Even if you are with a friend or two, don't go off with a stranger at night…no matter how cute he or she is. You can always meet the next day in broad daylight.

12. If you do think you are being followed, stop and duck into a public place to ask for help. Or, if you are in an area where you can hail a taxi, step out into the street and do so. Do NOT walk back to your hotel or apartment.

13. Don't take taxis that aren't registered with the city. Look for the proper identification such as an emblem, or taxi light on the roof of the car, a radio, or a meter. When in doubt, don't get in the taxi. Stop into a business, a hotel, or a restaurant and ask them to call a taxi for you.

14. Call Uber (See Chapter Seven) or a taxi rather than public transport to go to a night club or to meet up with friends for social outing.

15. Keep money/credit cards in more than one location on your person. Maybe in your purse or wallet and a second place: money belt or front zippered pocket in your pants or jacket. On the outside chance you are robbed, the thief is unlikely to find every area where you have stored money.

16. Be sure to carry a sturdy bag or backpack with hefty straps. Avoid carrying a clutch. Sling your purse with a strap across your body.

17. Don't over serve yourself. Too much alcohol is bad under any circumstance. And, remember, some countries serve stronger, more potent drinks. You want to be alert and aware of your surroundings at all times. Also, over drinking can alerting savory types that your alertness may be compromised. Not smart.

18. Never leave your drink unattended.

19. Lock doors and windows. Sometimes you may not lock up at home in your own house. It's easy to forget to lock your windows and doors. Also, pull shades and blinds so that others cannot see inside.

20. Wear small, costume jewelry or no jewelry at all.

21. If you choose to wear a cocktail dress or a low cut blouse, I question your critical thinking skills. Still, if you are dead certain with your choice, wear a cover up or coat until to get to your destination.

22. Join a tour group or meet up with friends of friends rather than going completely alone.

23. If you're traveling alone or in a small group, try to meet people during the day before going out rather than at night.

24. Keep your friends and family posted on where you are. Inform them of your location at all times. If you change your location, let them know immediately.

25. Trust your inner voice. It is always right. You need to make sure you are open to hearing it and acting accordingly.

Now that you know all these tips and follow them, you can feel comfortable enjoy yourself!

The Essential to a Life of Travel

Vignette: Prague

I traveled for over four house by train from Vienna, Austria, to Prague. I certainly needed the rest. After all, I had wandered the streets of Vienna, searching for live music and longing for fabulous architecture. And, yes, the Vienna music and architecture were beautiful, but, personally the design in Portugal and Spain is exquisite, more my cup of tea. Could it be that I am now satiated with astonishing sights, sounds, smells and tastes of eight months abroad? Oh, please, Desna, the goddess of travel and journey, say it isn't so!

I arrived at Praha Hlavni Nadrazi, the busiest train station in all of the Czech Republic, and walked for thirty minutes over the Lisbon-like pavement to my Airbnb apartment. I was not easy. The wheels of my suitcase jammed into the pavement every few feet, causing me to stop, turn, and adjust before beginning again.

Finally, I reached my destination and my non-English speaking host, the tall and beautiful Marketa, greeted me with fantastic exuberance. Her bright blue eyes lit up even brighter when she saw my guitar.

She spoke Czech interspersed with English and asked me to play something. I'm always ready to play and sing. I was happy to oblige and played "Blackbird" by the Beatles while she used her cell phone to video.

We sat at the table for some wine and cheese and managed to have a conversation. I learned that this fiftyish blonde woman had three daughters in their 20's, two granddaughters, and had been married for thirty-seven years, when her husband left her for a twenty-something woman, just five months prior.

I barely detected her sadness, but, when I touched her hand, she seemed to be more willing to let down her guard. Her pain was unmistakable.

Women are women, all over the world.

We sat in silence for the next ten minutes.

We finished our wine and quietly cried together for a few minutes longer. We hugged and promised to stay in touch as she walked out the door.

Thanks to my prayer to Desna, the next four days were filled with typical mouth-gaping, tourist-like awe. I let loose, oohing and ahhing, craning my already painful neck, tripping over lava stone slabs, mesmerized by it all...the Charles Bridge with its thirty mostly baroque statues and statuaries. The Vltava River (the longest in the country at 270 miles) was incredible with lovely swans skimming along the top of the water.

I saw astonishing castles and palaces, gold tipped towers and cathedrals, and sculptures crowning everything, everywhere. For the last one thousand years, the City of "100 bridges" has been the shining example of Romanesque, Gothic, Renaissance and Baroque architecture.

And, oh, the music....the live music, from jazz to folk to classical, is found everywhere, on the streets and bridges, in the churches, and in pubs and restaurants.

Getting around town was uncomplicated and varied from metro, tram, bus, taxi, rented bicycles and Segway's, motorcycles, scooters, self-peddled and electric skateboards, and on-your-own power.

Czech food is mostly pork or beef with sauce with a side dish of "knedliky," dumplings made from wheat or potato flour, boiled in water as a roll and then sliced and served hot. Chicken, duck, turkey, fish rabbit and lamb are prevalent. And, beer, beer, beer! The house red wine, my beverage of choice, was excellent and sells for as little as eighty cents a glass.

And, lots of ice cream, everywhere, served in warm sugar coated, freshly baked cylindrical cones. How could I resist? Well, I couldn't. I met an older gentleman, an Egyptian, man and we indulged on more than one occasions!

Thank you, Desna, oh goddess of travel and journey. Thank you for not deserting me!

CHAPTER NINE

Healthy Travel

Introduction
Guidelines for Healthy Travel
Exercise Apps

Traveling is medicine for the heart and the soul, but as anyone who's caught the wanderlust bug knows, it's not always glamorous. Many grand adventures, especially when venturing off-the-beaten-path come with their fair share of bumps, bruises, germs and stresses. It can be overwhelming and even intimidating when you begin to imagine how it will be to leave life's comforts at home.

But thankfully, wellness travel is possible, for sure! To help keep your mind, body and spirit in full working order, I have some guidelines for you.

Guidelines for Healthy Travel

1. See a doctor first. This is always good practice, especially if you are under a doctor's care, of course. And, seeing your doctor is especially important if you are a little older than the average free-spirited traveler.

2. Refill all your prescriptions and consider taking more than you will need, just in case you lose some or you end up extending your trip. Be sure to take specific information about your prescriptions with you, i.e., name, dosage, etc. Generally, you can get prescriptions filled most anywhere, unless of course you are alone in a desert or on a remote island. Still, you want to be ready for anything.

3. Always keep you medication in your purse or your backpack. Don't pack in your checked luggage in case it gets lost.

4. Bone up on your basic first aid. This is most important especially if you plan to visit in less developed countries. But, you might decide to venture out in the countryside. You never know when it might come in handy.

5. Take your vitamins. Travel is taxing. Take care of yourself. Stick with your vitamin regimen.

6. Eat healthy. This takes discipline, but, it is so important. You want to feel good all the time. Too much sugar, for example, can zap your energy and strain your system. And, wow, that pizza! I swear pizza dough rises again in my stomach! And, watch your salt intake, too. Check out the MyFitnessPal App in the next section of this Chapter to keep track of food intake.

7. Don't over serve yourself. I know what you are thinking. Just like me, the wine is wonderful and so many cultures start with a glass at lunch! Besides feeling woozy and needing a nap, the calories really add up. Remember: enjoy in moderation!

8. Eat your fiber! If you don't pay attention and eat your fiber, you could find yourself alone in a lavatory for much too long. Pack a natural laxative, just in case.

9. Wash your hands, frequently. Avoid dodgy food situations. Take hand sanitizer with you. With all that dancing, touching, kissing and hugging, you need to pay special attention to fight germs.

10. Stay hydrated. Drink lots of water, much more than you typically drink at home. Make it a habit to take a bottle with

    you whenever you walk out the door, even if it's for a short trip. You never knew where you might decide to venture off to see something wonderful. If you forget, buy a bottle as soon as you remember and be sure to remember to drink it.

11. Walk, walk, walk. Walking is easy and great exercise. Yes, a taxi is cheap and fast, but you can miss a lot of interesting sights by whizzing by in a car. Take your time and walk.

12. Hiking is the best workout. It is beneficial to the body, to the mind, and to the soul. If you have the right clothing and shoes, hike! And, breathe in great fresh air. Get your heart rate up, not only by moving your feet, but also by finding a breathtaking view.

13. Workout while traveling. If you aren't walking or hiking very much, you need to find some time to build up a good, healthy sweat. Check out the Exercise Apps in Chapter Nine. Download one or two that you know you will use!

14. Learn some basic meditation techniques. Traveling can be very stressful. Admit it, you often are out of your comfort zone, in a strange country, where, often, everything is totally different. Even when everything is wonderful, it can create stress...good stress, of course...but, stress, none the less. You don't have to become a monk or change your life style. Simply take time to channel some inner peace into their weary bones and tissues.

15. Embrace the sun light. The sun literally gives us life. Going out of your way to be surrounded by as much natural light as possible on your travels will enhance your spirits and warm your body and soul. Be sure to apply that sunblock!

16. Coconut oil is your friend. Using coconut oil is a really easy and travel-friendly way to keep your skin feeling nourished and fresh while on the road, especially when you are in that dry airplane air or in walking high altitudes.

17. Pace yourself. Don't overwhelm yourself and get burned out. Balance your activity with down time. Include down time in your daily calendar.

18. Sleep! You need it, especially when bombarded by fantastic everything! Take time to prepare for sleep…no radio, television, or internet. Perhaps, soothing conversation and light reading. When you do close your eyes, you mind will be prepared for sleep.

19. Pack lighter. When it really comes down to it, you probably won't need to bring anywhere close to the amount of stuff you think you'll need. Shed the pounds of luggage that crimp your back and shoulder muscles, slow you down, and make your more tired than need be.

20. Stay connected. Reach out to family and friends over Skype, Viber, or WhatsApp. (See Chapter Six.)

21. Go off the digital grid! Consider shutting down your digitals, for at least once a day. You will find how your mind can calm when not buried in your phone or in the internet news. Never fear, it will still will all be there when you return. Take this travel opportunity to focus on yourself and your adventure. Nurture your spirit. Let travel seep in and transform you into your even better self.

22. Open your mind and heart. Seriously, if you take a closer look, that's probably part of what drives you to travel. Indeed, travel is about the incredible architecture, the vast oceans and seas, the spectacular mountains, the inspirational music, and the people...especially the people. And, it is your opportunity to be who exactly you are, to be free of the well-intended expectations of your family and friends. Embrace this realization and open your heart and your mind to experiencing other cultures. All of this travelling and time for introspection stamps out prejudice and brings peace and understanding.

23. WRITE! Take some time to write. Of course, I'm an author and value the benefits of writing, perhaps more than non-writers. Still, I'm compelled to encourage you to write because you come to understand what you feel and what you know when you write. Write about your adventures, your new friends...capture your memories for later consumption. It's so good for getting inside yourself, finding creativity, and recording you adventures.

24. Indulge yourself! Live a little! Traveling is transformative. Allow yourself to experience it. Dance, sing, eat, and drink. Most important, let it saturate your mind and your body, even your pores.

Exercise Apps

Don't you just love eating foods from all over the world? And, the wines, I love the wines! Everything seems to taste even better when sitting at an outdoor restaurant on the Adriatic Sea in Dubrovnik, cruising the Danube, or at a Fado performance in Lisbon. But, the truth is all this scrumptious cuisine can really add up — and not just your credit card balance, but also calories and your waistline.

Don't you just hate it when those pants or that dress starts shrinking? I usually beat myself up afterwards, especially when I can't sleep because I'm so miserably stuffed! I also swear I will not repeat my over indulgence. But, when my diet is out of control, I continue to over serve myself with food and with drink.

Perhaps you are among the active travelers who hike or go on backpacking adventures. For me, I play tennis but it can be difficult to find courts or other players to join me. The answer? Well, guess what! There's an app for that!

Below are some popular workout apps to help whip you into shape or keep you in tip-top performance.

DailyBurn: Stream over 600 amazing workouts taught by expert, certified trainers. Whether you're a beginner or more advanced, whether you have 15 minutes or 1 hour, there's a workout for you.

MapMyRun: One of the best ways to explore every nook and cranny of a city is to run! With MapMyRun, you're able to procure a searchable list of routes in your destination city. As a result, you can go on runs like a "National Monument Five-Miler" when in Washington, D.C., or an "Art Run" in Paris. Once you start your workout, you can view anything from the amount of calories burned to elevation climbed. The paid version offers more in the way of training plans, as well as more detailed maps. Note: Requires WIFI/roaming.

MyFitnessPal: Do you worry about calorie consumption when traveling? Well, this app will track your calories. And, you can create a personal food diary and see what you've been consuming over the course of your cruise or South American adventure. You will see pretty quickly where your habits are sky rocketing your caloric intake, lacking of important minerals and nutrients, creating over-the-top sugar high, and more. The other benefit to MyFitnessPal is the multitude of exercises it keeps track of — more than 350 — so after logging your workouts, those food diaries won't make you feel so bad.

Nike Training Club: For exercise fiends who need some extra inspiration, Nike Training Club is just what the doctor ordered, and then some. The app gives you the opportunity to select workouts ranging from 15-45 minutes, and you can choose between low, medium and high-intensity levels depending on your mood that day. Nike recently debuted a new interface earlier this month that demonstrates videos of how to perform specific workouts as well so you don't lose form in the middle of a high-intensity workout.

Pocket Yoga: There are times when a long run or a weightlifting session at the gym just isn't practical and you need a good stretch and some meditation. Pocket Yoga contains more than 200 different poses designed by experienced yoga instructors and lets you unlock new features as you progress in your yoga journey. It costs $2.99, but this yoga app beats the $150 you might end up spending in a gym or a yoga studio.

SixPack App Pro: For serious fitness, this app has specialized travel workouts, focusing on your core. Instructions for each exercise ensure you have the correct posture and movements so you don't pull something while on a tour. (Cost: 99 cents)

Sworkit: Known as the so-called "Spotify" of workout apps, Sworkit comes in a free version, which contains more than 20 pre-built workouts that let you focus on yoga, cardio, stretching or strength training. The paid version, for $3.99 per month, entitles you to create custom workouts and gives you the support of a trainer, while also providing age-specific exercises for older adults.

Yep, sorry, but no more excuses!

Diann Schindler, Ph.D.

CHAPTER TEN

Luggage and Contents

Introduction
Carry-On Luggage Requirements for International Flights
Checked Baggage Requirements for International Flights
Now, you have asked me....
     What is in my suitcase?
     Two cabin bags
     What I do not pack
     Confession

Carry-on Luggage:
Size and Weight Restrictions
for International Flights

Generally, all airlines put a limit of 7kg (15.4 pounds) for hand luggage. A few allow for slightly more, but the standout airlines in this regard are British Airways which lets you take on 23kg 50.7 pounds) (so long as you can put the bag in the overhead lockers unassisted) and United which has no weight limit.

Nearly all airlines allow you one bag plus a smaller one, such as a handbag or laptop bag. China Airlines and Emirates, however, make no mention of a second bag on their websites, while Tigerair Australia simply says passengers are allowed two bags on with them (weight and sizing restriction apply).

The size of bags you're allowed to carry-on vary from airline to airline,

although there are a few dimensions that occur more than once. From the airlines checked, Thai Airways was the most spacious, allowing bags of 56cm x 45cm x 25cm onboard.

The table below, provided by SkyScanner,* lists the full details of each airline for you to compare and check prior to packing.

Airline	Allowance	Max. Dimensions*	Max. Weight
Air Asia	1 cabin bag+1 pers item	56cm x 36cm x 23cm	7kg
Air New Zealand	1 cabin bag+1 pers item	Sum of length, width & height must not measure more than a combined 118cm	7kg
British Airways	1 cabin bag+1 pers item	56cm x 45cm x 25cm	23kg
Cathay Pacific	1 cabin bag+1 pers item	56cm x 36cm x 23cm	7kg
China Airlines	1 cabin bag	56cm x 36cm x 23cm	7kg
Emirates	1 cabin bag	55cm x 38cm x 20cm	7kg
Etihad Airways	1 cabin bag+1 pers item	40cm x 50cm x 25cm	7kg
Fiji Airways	1 cabin bag+1 pers item	55cm x40cm x 23cm	7kg
Garuda Indonesia	1 cabin bag + 1 personal item	56cm x 36cm x 23cm	7kg
Japan Airlines	1 cabin bag+1 pers item	55cm x 40cm x 25cm	10kg
Jetstar	1 cabin bag+1 pers item	55cm x 36cm x 23cm	7kg
KLM	1 cabin bag	55cm x 35cm x 25cm	12kg
Lufthansa	1 cabin bag+1 pers item	55cm x 40cm x 23cm	8kg
Malaysia Airlines	1 cabin bag+1 pers item	55cm x 35cm x 25cm	7kg
Qantas	1 cabin bag+1 pers item	48cm x 34cm x 23cm	7kg
Qatar Airways	1 cabin bag+1 pers item	50cm x 37cm x 25cm	7kg
Scoot	1 cabin bag+1 pers item	54 x 38 x 23 cm	7kg
Singapore Airlines	1 cabin bag+1 pers item	Sum of length, width & height must not measure more than a combined 115cm	7kg
Thai Airways	1 cabin bag+1 pers item	56cm x 45cm x 25cm	7kg
Tigerair	2 bags	54cm x 38cm x 23cm	7kg
United	1 cabin bag+1 pers item	56cm x 35cm x 22cm	No weight limit
Virgin Australia	1 cabin bag+1 pers item	48cm x 34cm x 23cm	7kg

Personal items include handbag, briefcase, laptop computer, camera bag, crutches, umbrella, etc

*one cm = .39 inches Therefore, 56cm = 22 inches; 36cm = 14 inches; 23ch = 9 inches.

*Source: www.skyscanner.net/news/cabin-luggage-guide-hand-baggage-sizes-and-weight-restrictions

When travelling with hand luggage alone, it's important to remember restrictions on liquids and other prohibited items.

Checked Baggage Requirements for International Flights

Rules for luggage continue to change for both domestic and international flights depending on current safety concerns. Baggage requirements for international airline travel are usually stricter than those for domestic flights, with countries and airlines often enforcing rules of their own.

Checked Bags: Most airlines allow two checked bags weighing between 50 and 70 lbs., depending on the airline, when flying to or from the United States. Outside the U.S., the limit for checked bags is either 20kg (44 pounds) or 23kg (50.7 pounds, according to the carrier. Airlines from other countries, especially the smaller carriers, use a weight system that might add the weight of your carry-on to your checked baggage. The weight system is very restrictive compared, sometimes allowing luggage no heavier than 22 lbs. Always check your international plane tickets to see which system is being used.

Luggage Size and Individual Airlines: Some international airlines have different size, pound and piece restrictions based on fare class and/or travel zones. Overall, the average weight and size for checked bags is 50 pounds and 62 inches. An average maximum size for carry-on luggage is 45 inches. Luggage is always measured by adding length, width and height, including handles and wheels.

Final notes:

1. Check with your airline for its most current restrictions and policies and TSA guidelines for banned or prohibited items. And, given the recent changes regarding laptops, always check these guidelines before purchasing tickets.

2. Check with your airline for any additional restrictions for individual nations.

3. Do not lock your baggage unless you have purchased the locks from airports or travel stores that use the "universal master key," so that TSA security personnel can open your bags.

4. If you are unsure if an item should be in your carry-on, put it in your checked luggage to avoid possibly having to throw the item away at security check point

Now, you have asked me....

One of the reasons for writing this book was because I was asked so many questions about travel, and most of those questions are about packing. Specifically, because I carry everything I own, what do I have in my suitcase?

I assume that most of you reading this book are not planning to sell all your possessions and become a nomad, as I did. As noted earlier, I have no car and I have no home. And, I have no storage units!

As a result, the following information can be considered a severe approach to packing. If you follow these guidelines, you can probably add items to your luggage, for sure.

But, you asked....

I began by purging, big time! I weeded through all my clothes, giving unwanted items to charities, selling lots at a yard sale, giving stuff to my daughter, dropping off items to my favorite consignment shop, and simply pitching loads more! I also sold a few things on EBay and Craig's List.

Finally, I was down to the bare minimum and ready to organize. To that end, I now have only the basics:

<u>One suitcase</u>, long enough to accommodate my tennis racket and packed with clothing and essentials not to exceed the typical 23 kilograms or 50.7 pounds. As noted earlier, some smaller airlines have a limit of limit of 20 kilograms. I have two choices: either purge more or get creative and shift items from my suitcase to my back pack.

Plus, I try to avoid those airlines that add the weight of your carry-on and your checked bag together to determine an overall weight limit. While I have flown on airlines that say they do that, none have ever actually weighed both. I guess, it's bound to happen someday, but until then, I'm getting away with a little more than I should.

What is in My Suitcase?

I take only comfortable clothes. Comfortable means not tight anywhere AND I must feel good about myself when wearing them. That is, I can wear it anywhere without feeling self-conscience; not sheer, not low cut, not too short, not too flashy, not boring...you get my drift.

Also, clothing must be versatile, interchangeable. For example, the tops should work with jeans, pants, and the skirt.

Another consideration is the weather. I prefer the warmer climates, but when I do choose to visit the cold, I have my "coat in a bag." It's light weight with a thin down lining and a hood. I avoid buying a real winter coat and opt for layering instead.

The following goes into my checked suitcase, 12"x28"x20," 23 kilograms or 50.7 pounds.

- one pair of jeans
- two pairs of slacks
- two pairs of leggings (one pair heavyweight and one pair lightweight)
- five pairs of panties
- five tops

- three bras plus a running bra
- one pair of tennis shorts
- one tennis top
- one hoodie
- two dresses
- bathing suit
- one skirt
- two scarves
- two sweaters
- lightweight raincoat with a hood
- a "coat in a bag" with a hood
- shoes: One of each: all-season boots, sandals, heels, tennis shoes, running shoes, and flip flops.
- tennis racket
- health and beauty items: Bag of essential make up items, olive-oil based bar soap, brush, comb, hair gel, emery boards, toe nail clippers, and sometimes hairspray (according to the length of my hair at the time).
- umbrella
- day back pack

Two cabin bags

I carry on m 7/8 Baby Taylor guitar. I have successfully taken my guitar abroad without an extra fee throughout my travels, save two: Germania and Ryanair.

Also, I have a large backpack. I pack those items I must have when in transit, including things I don't want to "lose" in my checked baggage:

- personal items: toothbrush, tooth paste, ibuprofen, vitamins, tissue and wipes
- jewelry (costume)
- reading glasses (2) and sun glasses

electronics: My laptop, camera, phone jacks, one converter for electrical outlet camera, computer, microphone and earphones for podcasting, phone jack and external battery pack.

What I Do Not Take

- cologne (Soaps, creams and shampoos already have enough fragrance.)
- fingernail polish and remover. I buy it when I need and leave it in the hotel room or apartment.
- hair dryer - most places provide one.

Confession!

I confess, clothing is my downfall and, as much as I fight it, I am completely drawn to the style of the country in which I am visiting. Paris was crazy expensive! And, I loved the colorful clothing and bags throughout South America.

Shoes! Oh, my gosh, shoes!! Yep, I want to buy shoes everywhere! I fell in love with the over-the-top platform slides in Buenos Aires. (I somehow resisted. And, it's good that I did. They are so heavy and not good for walking over the treacherous, uneven streets of Europe.)

I find myself doing a lot of window shopping, all the while talking myself out of buying.

How have I coped? First, I am no longer in denial. I have identified and admitted I have a disease! Also, it helps, but only somewhat, to know that if my suitcase weight exceeds the guidelines, I will waste money…extra fees up to $50! Plus, 50 pounds, along with my backpack and guitar is a heavy load to carry. It can be painful wear and tear on my body, if I give in to my addiction.

I manage by window shopping and put off purchasing. I tell myself that I can buy those shoes tomorrow, not today. I have only returned to the store once to buy those shoes, and by then, they were out of stock! Yay!

I do not deny myself completely, however. If I am compelled to buy, if I just can't help myself, I go through my clothing in my mind to see what I can give up by giving to a local second-hand store or, simply pitch.

Honestly, my gotta-have-it clothing syndrome is never ending.

(I thought writing this confession, acknowledging my dysfunction to my reader, world would help my condition. I'll let you know!)

Vignette: San Sebastián, Spain

San Sebastián was overcast and dreary my first day. I arrived at my hotel late in the evening, after a twelve-hour day on a series of trains all the way from Gandia, Spain. I was still recuperating from two wonderful weeks of fun, frolic, food, and music with my friends in Oliva and weary from the full-day train ride, which included three transfers and a taxi.

My hotel was just six blocks away and I certainly over paid taxi driver the 7.20 euros. But, it was worth being escorted in a strange city at the end of night.

After a few minutes settling in my room in an ancient hotel, brimming with culture, I washed my face, brushed my teeth, fell into bed and was in deep sleep instantly.

The next morning, I walked to a nearby upscale cafe. I scanned the interior to see an impressive bar, lined with luscious tapas. The deep brown brick walls contrasted beautifully with the dark green framed windows which provided a dazzling view of exquisite architecture of every square meter of this famously romantic city. Barely audible music, "Blue Monday" by Nouvelle Vague, added to the ambiance.

I sat at the first open table and waited to be served. Then, I waited, at least to be acknowledged. And, I waited longer. I realized that I had been remiss. This lovely café required customers to step up to the bar and place an order...probably the usual custom in this community so close to the French border.

I stood at the counter and was totally ignored by the very attractive young woman and 40-something male manager. Soon, from behind me, a man entered the front door and both employees looked up and greeted him with inviting smiles. I assumed this fella was a regular. But, I also needed breakfast and quickly smiled, "Hola, solo cafe and croissant, por favor?"

They both nodded and began making a coffee, not from a pot of coffee, but in an elaborate one-cup-at-a-time machine. My caffeine need was near paralyzing. Just as the woman turned toward me with a java filled cup in her hands, I leaned forward to take the cup from her. Ah, but, no, she turned, just slightly and handed it to the gentleman.

I smiled pleasantly and waited longer. And, it wasn't easy, believe me. Oh, so how I wanted to turn into the "ugly American."

Finally, the manager handed me my order. I carried it to my table, sat, and drank. It was just what I needed. My brain cleared and my stomach settled.

Now, I was able to look around the café and see my fellow patrons. A well-dressed group of people, saw that they that were sitting and waiting for someone to take their orders.

"Aha," I said to myself, "they will learn, just as I did."

Just then, the waitress passed my table and took the order of three older women at a table next to me. Then, she went to the two gentlemen, then the couple, until she had taken the orders from everyone sitting in the café.

"Humph!" I thought. "The stereotypical French influence!"

I wondered if I would he faced with lack of attention and little kindness throughout my three days in San Sebastián.

Undeterred, however, I ate, paid a mere 5.50 euros (no tip) with a nice smile, a pleasant "muchas gracias," prepared my camera, and began my own walking tour of the city.

It was Easter Monday. Note: Spaniards celebrate holidays with a holiday a day before that actual holiday, the holiday, and also another holiday to recuperating from celebrating the holiday. A total of three days. A superb custom, I might add.

I found only pharmacies and restaurants open for business. The promenade near the sea was magnificent with tourists and locals strolling often arm in arm or hand in hand, with their families and pooches....everything from delicate Pomeranians to Bulldogs and slobbering Mastiffs. Honestly, it all was breathtaking and right out of a vintage Hollywood movie, especially with a lone trumpeter playing "Besame Mucho," accompanied with delicate background music.

111

It was 15 degrees C...that's 59 degree F... and yet young men in their tight wetsuits surfed and kayaked, while four die-hard seniors waded up to their bellies...and I mean bellies... in the cool water. Waves crashed loudly against the barrier walls, protecting the Passarella and series of light brown and terracotta toned buildings that surrounded this gorgeous, massive beach.

Little girls and boys rode the astonishingly ornate pink and gold carousel, blinking festive with bright lights and playing the traditional Walter Rolfe's 1925 "Moon Rocket," on the pipe organ. Childhood memories came flooding back to me.

I took another direction, walking toward even more impressive buildings near incredible old hotels, adorned in brilliant bright red, pink, blue and yellow flowers, with dark green hedges, groomed with sharp angles. I found yet another magnificent promenade, lined on both sides with an opulent, white iron railing that backed inland away from the sea inlet as far as my eyes could see.

And, yes, I heard more music. I followed my ears. It was opera music.

Be still, my heart!

Right there in the street, encircled with amazed onlookers was a stand-up bass, a trumpet and clarinet and an incredible young singer with a pristine, strong voice and the stage presence of a professional, way beyond her years.

I was moved to tears.

I felt my initial breakfast experience shimmered away into nothingness. I found a café within ear shot and order wine.

A glass of vinho tinto completed my utopian introduction to San Sebastián.

CHAPTER ELEVEN

Multiple-Destination Trip Planning

Introduction
Useful Websites for Multi-City Trips
When to Go: Know Your Seasons
        What is HIGH season, LOW season,
                and SHOULDER season?
        Specific Locations and Seasons
Limit Destinations
Travel Overland, by Train or Bus
Hub Cities

Introduction

You want to plan a multi-city trip? It seems so complicated. This Chapter focuses on multi-city trip planning and when is the best time of year to go? Also, how to make this complex and fabulous vacation more affordable.

Useful Websites for Multi-City Trips

The world's a big place and you don't have to try to see it all at once. To avoid driving yourself crazy, check those travel booking websites I mentioned earlier in Chapter One. Especially, check with Airtrek, Secret Flying, and Flynous.

After you done general research and come up with a couple of plans, take the time to call them and ask for help.

Let's go over a few ways to make your trip more affordable.

When to Go: Know Your Seasons

The first question is simply **when** should you go? I know, I know. No matter the season, you only have the time you have to get away, especially if you are working and if you have family. If you are retired, it should be easier.

As you probably know, traveling during busy times can increase your costs. But did you know the costs can go up as much as 30 percent or more during high season? That's a huge increase, actually. Let's take a moment to discuss the seasons, in general.

What is HIGH season,
what is LOW season
and, what is SHOULDER season?

High season: Late December through early January is high season because of Christmas and New Year's, a time when many people visit friends and family. The seasonality factor is especially relevant traveling to or from high-traffic, seasonal destinations like Europe, Asia, and the South Pacific. Then, of course, summer (June 15 to Sept 21 or so) is high season in most temperate zones North America and Europe.

Remember, though, summer in the southern hemisphere (Australia, New Zealand, and South America) is the opposite and means, roughly, November to February.

Low Season: In most places, better bargains are available during the low season. As a rule, you will experience lower transportation and lodging fees. And, even better, you will see fewer people, fewer lines and less waiting time.

Winter, from about January 10th to March 31st, is the low season (ski resorts excepted), with lower rates and fewer crowds (and, obviously, colder weather).

Still, I love Paris or Venice in February when the air is crisp air and most tourists stay home. I love wearing my classy, cozy black leather boots I bought in Istanbul in 2015. And, what's more, the sales in the stores are fantastic!

And, again, it's the opposite in the southern hemisphere.

Shoulder season: This season is between low and high. It's not winter and not summer, but spring and fall, when crowds are thinner, prices are not quite as high, and the weather can be mild. I say CAN be because even spring and fall can turn cold and wet. Be prepared. Of course, more people are traveling during shoulder season in the last few years, due to books, like this one, touting shoulder season travel. The good news is that cost of flights is still slightly lower, at least this is true at the time of this writing.

Specific Locations and Seasons

Beach destinations and the Caribbean: Popular beach destinations mark the high season when the tourists are escaping their own weather conditions. That is to say, winter in North America is high season for the Caribbean. Low season for the Caribbean is the June to November. But, and this is something to consider, June to November is "hurricane season."

Yet, the islands well south of the hurricane belt, such as the Netherlands Antilles (Aruba, Bonaire, and Curacao) see fewer tourists. Of course, the obvious benefit is less likelihood of hurricanes.

The tropics: In semi-tropical and tropical destinations, a smart choice is to visit during the dry season, rather than the rainy season. The dry season is very hot, of course, and also humid!

There is a reason snowbirds flick back north from Florida in summer. Have you ever been there in August? I lived there and take it from me, it's barely semi-tropical!

Then there is Southeast Asia. This area of the world includes countries south of China, east of India and north of Australia. Western travelers may choose to immerse themselves in big cities like Bangkok, Singapore and Kuala Lumpur, or quiet paradises in Bali, Laos and Thailand. The best time to visit countries like Vietnam, Cambodia, Malaysia and the Philippines largely depends upon skipping the hottest and most humid weather, as well as the swelling crowds.

November through February is generally the best. It's drier, cooler. Average temperatures are about 80 degrees F, all year round. The hottest is March to June with temperatures up to 97 degrees. June to October is the monsoon season for all these countries, except for Malaysia and Indonesia. Their dry season is from April to October. But, watch those fares. They can climb during these months.

The tourist season in Southeast Asia is November to February and includes higher flight and hotel fees and hordes of people. Honestly, the best time to travel is in April and May. (However, avoid visiting during the early April New Year celebrations in Thailand and Laos.) And, yes, it is hot. Be prepared.

Southeast Asia is incredibly affordable, especially in Indonesia, Laos and Cambodia. Despite the affordability of the region, there are certain times to stretch your dollar even further. The summer months may be stiflingly hot, but flight and hotel deals are fairly cheap to places like Vietnam and Thailand. September and October are cheaper times to fly because they precede the busy travel season.

Limit Destinations

As noted above, if you want to go around the world, check out Airtrek (page 4) for sure and be aware that round-the-world ticket fares are usually based on miles traveled. Therefore, the more destinations, the higher the "round the world" ticket(s) price, especially when you cross oceans.

Consider visiting fewer destinations, especially when planning a multi-destination trip. This will save money and you will have more time to explore each destination. Personally, this would work for me. I prefer more in-depth knowledge of a destination I'm visiting.

If you work with Trip Planner on Airtrek (Chapter One), you can plan to see more places and turn those time-wasting layovers into fun and informative stopovers.

Travel Overland by Train or Bus.

I'm sold on train travel after traveling the ancient Feve train, for two weeks, all the way across northern Spain. It was beautiful and so inexpensive that I'm embarrassed to tell you cost! (Well, I did confess the cost in *Vignette: The Feve*, Chapter One).

I love overland travel because I can escape the flashy fast-paced cities by relaxing and seeing firsthand views of the beautiful countryside. Plus, it is less expensive.

I say, mix it up! Flashy cities to countryside and back again. Experience it all!

And, what a great way to break-up your modes of transportation, view more of the country, and save money, too!

Again, check out Rome2Rio (page 8) for all the details for train and bus travel.

Hub Cities

Fly in and out of hub-cities whenever possible. It's always less expensive. Don't know the hub cities? It's usually the country's capital or biggest city since that's where the carrier will connect to smaller cities or towns in the country.

But, don't leave it up to chance. Find out for sure by accessing Wikipedia's List of Hub Cities.
https://en.wikipedia.org/wiki/List_of_hub_airports

Vignette: Fez, Morocco

It was 9 am and we were all in the lobby ready to board the bus to tour Fez for the day. Dorine and Shirley from the Philly area, my friends of friends, had invited me via Facebook to join them on a 7-day tour of Morocco. I was ecstatic. I shortened my two weeks in Barcelona by one week to meet them, for the first time, in Malaga.

The next morning, we boarded a ferry to Tangier for quick half day bus tour and arrived in Fez. We picked up Marta and Sylvia, two well-travelled, smart, successful young women from Lisbon, Portugal.

Our driver and tour guide, Jahlil, helped us into the van. Just at the last moment, an attractive, dark woman with black eyes, beautifully rimmed with just the right amount of black eye liner, full pale lips, a lovely smile, gracefully entered the bus. Black boots, tights, the hood of the Logan green winter coat, cinched at her narrow waist, surrounded her dark brown hair. She was beautiful with a warm personality that became evident as she introduced herself as Milly, our Fez tour guide.

A gust of wind and rain blew through the van door opening. Milly quickly reached in her bag, pulled out a knitted cap and slipped it over her head. Yes, now, she was stunning.

Founded in the 9th century and home to the oldest university in the world, Fez reached its height in the 13th–14th centuries under the Marinids, when it replaced Marrakesh as the capital of the kingdom. The urban fabric and the principal monuments in the medina – madrasas, fondouks, palaces, residences, mosques and fountains - date from this period. Although the political capital of Morocco was transferred to Rabat in 1912, Fez has retained its status as the country's cultural and spiritual centre.

She took us into the Medina, the ancient marketplace of Fez.

"There are 9500 streets, some so narrow and so shallow it is difficult to walk, in the Medina. But, I grew up here and know them all. Watch me carefully and follow up. It is easy to get lost. Stay close to me at all times," Milly said.

We tagged along like dutiful children while she shared little known information about this wonderful place. We were mesmerized with the smells of spices, honey, cigarettes and leather. We tasted spices and rubbed concoctions on our hands and face. Motorbikes attached to small truck beds careened through the streets, popping exhaust and demanding their space in the marketplace. We turned sideways to walk through narrow streets, less than 18 inches wide.

We all were curious about Milly and her life here in this third-world country that has little respect for women. She explained that she married in a civil ceremony three months ago. She had been confident, while they were dating, that her husband that he was a good match for her. However, since they were married she was not permitted to visit her family or travel. He had tricked her into believing he was supportive of her work and her travels.

Furthermore, her husband's family didn't want her to leave the area or visit her family because they thought her family would give her money and she would leave her husband. The official, religious marriage ceremony would occur in six weeks.

I asked why she would continue with the marriage and couldn't she leave before the religious ceremony. She explained that she was the oldest of nine children and all of her younger sisters were married. Her mother wanted her to marry. She wanted to please her mother and to ensure that her family no longer had to be ashamed that their oldest daughter was not married. She would go ahead with the ceremony.

All of us were saddened by this news about our tour guide who had in a few short hours become "our Milly." We loved her.

We discussed all angles, wanted to encourage her to leave, help her to get away, give her money to escape, take her away with us today.

"I am happy to please my mother, my family. I have shamed them and I must do the right thing, for them. I am fine."

This was the way it was.

The tour was to end at 2:30 that afternoon, but we asked Milly to continue with us throughout the afternoon. She obliged.

The rain continued, the wind was brutal, our feet got cold and wet, and water seeped through our clothes. We shivered in the cold and wet. But, we did not complain. How could we?

Our physical discomfort paled when we were with our lovely Milly. We all knew, without saying it. Milly would lead an extremely difficult life…a life she chose for the sake of her family.

At 5:30, we said good bye with hugs, kisses and generous tips. She knew how much we appreciated her work. And, our hearts broke for her.

We learned much more about Medina, Fez and Morocco that day.

CHAPTER TWELVE

Miscellaneous and Odd and Ends

Introduction
Immunizations
    Where to Find Travel Immunizations
    What Are the Costs?
    FindMyiPhone and FindMyPhone Apps
Driving Abroad
International Drivers' License
Driver Safety Abroad
Rental Car Insurance

Introduction

This Chapter lists those important odds and ends that do not naturally fit under the categories of the chapters of this book. Nonetheless, this is very important information to know: Immunizations, Driver Safety Abroad, International Driver's License, and Rental Car Insurance.

Immunizations

Remember to pack good health for your trip! Vaccines are your passport to adventure around the world. You may come into contact with different diseases based on the countries you are visiting. For example, you may need the yellow fever vaccine if traveling to certain countries in Africa, Central America, or South America. In addition, some vaccines may be required for you to travel to certain places or areas within a country. Protect yourself and your community by getting vaccinated before you travel.

Which vaccines do you need for your trip and when should you get vaccinated? Four to six weeks before you travel, make sure you are up-to-date on routine vaccinations and schedule an appointment with your health care provider to get the recommended vaccines for the countries you plan to visit. This gives the vaccines enough time to start working, time and treatment should you experience a bad reaction, and time for vaccines that require more than one dose.

Where to Find Travel Immunizations

Talk to your health care provider about recommended immunizations before you travel. Check with your local health department. Some health departments provide travel vaccines. But, be aware, not all health departments have all vaccines. When in you find a travel clinic in your area, call them and find out which vaccines they have and which are in stock. Don't assume anything. And, if you are pregnant or have any health issues, be sure to share that information so that any precautions are taken into consideration.

You can search the International Society of Travel Medicine (ISTM) for travel medicine specialists. The ISTM has a Global Clinic directory which lists clinics located in more than 90 countries, clinics offer pre-travel immunizations, counseling and medicines to help protect travelers while traveling internationally. Most clinics also provide care to travelers if needed upon their return. www.istm.org

Visit the Centers for Disease Control and Prevention (CDC) Travel Health site for details on vaccines and other important information to stay healthy while you travel. You can also download CDC's TravWell App, which helps users find out vaccine and medicine recommendations for each country. (See Chapter Seven.)

Finally, be sure to visit the CDC website. It has a wealth of information beyond immunizations. www.cdc.gov

What Are the Costs?

Travel vaccinations are not covered by Medicare or many private health insurance plans. According to Passport Health, which operates travel clinics across the United States, many health insurance plans do not cover vaccinations needed for travel because insurers consider them elective.

However, some plans do cover travel vaccinations. For example, most of Aetna's traditional plans that include preventive services cover medically necessary travel vaccinations. And some BlueCross BlueShield of Rhode Island plans cover travel vaccinations, but not initial consultations. For patients covered by health insurance, typical expenses include a co-pay of $10 to $40 for the doctor visit and a copay for the vaccination.

For patients whose health insurance doesn't cover immunizations for foreign travel, the cost of travel immunizations at a travel clinic typically includes an initial consultation fee of $15 to $100, a shot administration fee of $10 to $20 per shot, and the cost of the vaccines, which can range from less than $10 per dose to $150 or more per dose, depending on the disease. Some vaccinations require as many as three shots.

Travel vaccinations could range from less than $50 for one routine booster shot to $1,000 or more for several vaccinations, especially those that require multiple shots, such as rabies or Japanese Encephalitis.

As an example of a travel clinic fee schedule, the Michigan State University Travel Clinic charges consultation fees for non-students ranging from $35 for 15 minutes to $95 for an hour, and shot administration fees of $20 for the first shot and $15 for each additional shot.

In general, a typhoid vaccination typically costs $85 to $300 total; a meningococcal meningitis vaccination typically costs $100 to $150 total; a yellow fever vaccination typically costs $150 to $350 total; a

Japanese Encephalitis vaccination typically costs $450 to $800 total; and a rabies vaccination typically costs $500 to $1,000 total.

While the cost seems high, defense against possible long-term health challenges, or even death, is worth it.

Driver Safety Abroad

Are you thinking about driving in another country? If so, know that road conditions, laws, and driving norms in other countries can be very different from those in the United States. Poor road maintenance, lack of signs, vehicle safety, and insurance coverage are just some things you should consider. And, remember to buckle up, no matter where you are.

Read about road safety in your destination country before you go and keep these things in mind when planning your trip:

- Potential hazards and dangerous road conditions
- Local roads or areas to avoid
- Availability of roadside assistance
- Need for spare tires, fuel and a map
- Local laws and driving culture -- Get information from the country's embassy or consulates in the United States, foreign government tourism offices, or from a car rental company in the foreign country. Become aware of the rules of the roads, especially with regard to pedestrians.
- Local emergency numbers (See Chapter Seven.)
- Vehicle safety considerations, including seat belts
- Documents to carry, including any special road permits
- Insurance (See Chapter Three).

International Driving Permits

It is illegal to drive without a valid license and insurance in most countries. You should check with the embassy of the country you plan to visit or live in to find specific driver's license requirements. (For a list of links to the websites of U.S. Embassies, Consulates, and

Diplomatic Missions, by country, go to this link: www.usembassy.gov

Many countries do not recognize a U.S. driver's license, but most accept an International Driving Permit (IDP). And, note, IDP's may not be valid the whole time you stay abroad and usually is only valid with you U.S. License. Be sure to have both in your possession.

You can get an IDP at your local AAA (American Automobile Association). The fee generally runs at about $20.

Rental Car Insurance

The following paragraphs speak to the financial risks due to a traffic accident or collision and cover repair costs, loss-of-use charges, and more.

These plans also typically include roadside assistance benefits and cover both traveler-owned vehicles (as secondary automobile insurance) and rental vehicles (as secondary unless the traveler doesn't currently have automobile insurance, then the coverage becomes primary by default).

Car and rental car plans typically come with the following types of coverage:

• Coverage for repairs due to a collision, towing costs, and loss-of-use charges imposed by a rental car company
• Travel assistance services including roadside assistance while on a covered trip

Some plans have additional coverage for:

• Emergency medical expenses
• Trip interruptions
• Trip cancellations
• Travel delays
• Lost, stolen or destroyed baggage
• Travel accident accidental death and dismemberment

Be aware that driver protection and car rental insurance coverage offered at the car rental counter can be exorbitant. While coverage at the rental counter can be as high as $20 per day, this same coverage from insurance companies is typically $7 to $9 per day and includes coverage for loss-of-use charges imposed by the rental company if the vehicle is damaged.

Many car rental insurance companies exist but, first, check with your own auto insurance. If you can't buy what you want with your existing company ask your travel friends where they have found affordable and quality insurance and do some googling on your own.

Here are two I have used. They cater to travelers from all over the world. Both are known for their clarity when explaining options and their quality customer service.

Allianz Global Assistance is a reasonable and reputable company with good customer service. www.allianztravelinsurance.com/travel/rental-cars

iCarHireInsurance is physically located in the UK. But, everything you need to know is online. If you plan to rent a car in the Schengen Area, you want to look at this company. www.icarhireinsurance.com

Vignette: Krakow: A Capitulation

Alas, I must confess: I was leaving from Madeira Island, Portugal, working my way through Vienna, to Prague and finally landing in Krakow. For the first time, I used Owner's Direct for lodging.

I found a perfect apartment near the Old Town in Krakow. It was a one bedroom apartment with sleek black and white decor, an up-to-date bathroom, functional kitchen and WIFI, and big windows for lots of natural light. The price was a little steep, but it was during high season. I was willing to pay the additional cost.

Unfortunately, the only reasonably priced and short non-stop flight from Prague to Krakow arrived at 11:00 at night. I broke my own solo-female traveler cardinal rule: Be safe. Do not arrive at your location late at night.

It was what it was. I developed a plan to alleviate my concerns. I would use the taxi driver's help to ensure my safety.

Meanwhile, before I left Prague, just as always, I contacted my host, Ihar, through the Owner's Direct website for the exact address and to let her know I would be arriving late. She said it was at Lobzowska 53 Street and to text Allen, when I arrived. He would like me in.

(As you may know, when you book through Airbnb, Owner's Direct, and similar booking sites, you only know the general area of your rental location. The exact address is sent to you later by your host.)

When I arrived in Krakow, I approached the taxi stand and met a driver. He was about 40, blond, well dressed, with a nice smile. As he was putting my luggage in the boot, I explained that I didn't like arriving so late at night, especially when I was unfamiliar with the area. He nodded, handed me his card, shook my hand and said, "I am Petr. Welcome. Do not worry. I will see to it you are safe."

I began breathing easier.

As we drove away, I opened my Here GPS App, keyed in the address and watched the dot representing the taxi move along the route to my apartment.

We pulled up to the apartment address. Unfortunately, the lack of street light obscured our vision.

"This doesn't look good," Petr said.

"Wait, let me out for a closer look."

I stepped out onto the street. I managed, through tangled overgrown weeds and trees, to see ugly graffiti on the lower walls on what we thought might be the apartment building. Graffiti in Europe is often considered art. This was not art, trust me.

Petr called Allen for more instructions. Allen confirmed that we were at the correct location. A few minutes later, tall, lean twenty-something fellow greeted us.

Petr's facial expression was clear concern for me. After removing my luggage from the boot, he nodded indicating he would wait for me.

Allen unlocked the door. I was surprised. I didn't remember the mention of stairs in the description. He took my 45 pound suitcase up, not one flight of stairs, but four flights of cement steps. Thank goodness he was there to help or I might still be climbing with my hefty luggage.

Finally, we entered the apartment and, once again, my memory failed me. I didn't recall that the bed was behind the sofa in the living room. I decided Ihar must have rearranged the furniture and I quickly dismissed any concern.

Allen reached out his hand and said he needed payment for the apartment. I explained that I had already paid.

He asked for payment again. I pulled up my receipt on my phone and showed it to him.

He nodded an acceptance. But, kept his hand out and said I needed to pay him a "late arrival" fee. He said Ihar had called me and left a message about the fee.

"No one called me."

He repeated, "The late arrival fee is 51 zloty."

"I only have euros."

"Good. Fifty-one zloty is equal to 12 euros."

I exhaled in disgust and capitulated.

I gave him the money, walked him to the door, and down the stairs. Petr was leaning against his car.

I waved to him. He stood up, opened his arms as if to ask me if everything I alright. I nodded, blew a kiss and waved good-bye.

I climbed back up the stairs, entered my apartment, locked the door, brushed my teeth and fell into bed. It was 1:00 am. It had been a long, challenging day.

Happily, by morning, bright sunlight streamed through the windows in the kitchen and living room. I looked out to see a magnificent red brick Catholic Church, surrounded by gardens, brimming with red, pink, white, orange, and violet flowers. An old yellow dog was outstretched on the pavement with his head lazily perched on the bottom of an ornate iron fence. I was spellbound.

For the next two days, I walked for hours, visiting Old Town and the Schindler Museum, housed in his original factory where Oskar Schindler hired Jews and helped them escape. All the while, I kept thinking about those stairs and the church. Were the stairs mentioned in the description? Why wasn't this beautiful church pictured to lure renters?

I decided to check out the advertisement again. What I found was shocking!

Silence on any stairs and no picture of the church were the immediate clues. But, more, the apartment I had reserved and paid for had a new bathroom with gleaming sliding glass shower doors, one large room rather than the three in my current space, and much larger windows.

What really happened and how stupid could I be!

After berating myself for the next hour, I looked around, noting my dissatisfaction with my current apartment. I had just two bathroom towels; no kitchen towels; only used, ragged kitchen sponges; an old dilapidated, stained but functional refrigerator with cracked plastic shelves; no shower curtain over the tub; and just three rusty pans under the sink. I seethed.

I googled the website on the business card left on the coffee table. A "chat" popped up and a texting conversation began.

To make a long story longer, Aleksja said this was a "simple mistake" and I could move immediately. I ignored her offer to move and went on to question the "late arrival fee". She replied that she had emailed me a message about that. Of course, I noted that I did not receive an email message from her. Besides, Allen said he called and I had no records of her call either.

She didn't acknowledge my comment. Rather, she noted that I was currently in was more expensive than the one I had actually rented. (This was true. I had learned that from the company's website.)

I agreed. However, I added, in my experience, this apartment was overpriced. She ignored me and asked "what hour do you want to move?" I asked her to send me a copy of the email she sent me regarding the "late arrival" fee. She ignored that, as well, and repeated "what hour do you want to move?"

I responded that my trust for their organization was depleted as a result of their incorrect communication, lack of organization, and fabrication of email messages. Furthermore, it would take me all day to pack, move, and unpack. I didn't want to waste my time, especially since I was not confident I would be taken to the correct apartment. I asked again for a copy of the "late arrival" fee message.

The chat room abruptly closed.

How rude! This entire event was beyond annoying!

However, I truly did capitulate. What choice did I have?

But, what did I do wrong?   How did I contribute to this fiasco?

I went over it again and again and decided when I entered the apartment and wondered about the stairs and the placement of the bed and when Allen asked me for money, I should have protested.

Truth was, I doubt anyone else would be around to address my problem.   What good would that have done at my late arrival time?

Aha! That's it! My error was arriving too late at night...too late to do anything about it.

"Lesson learned!" I grumbled out loud.

But, there I was. I could choose to continue dwell on the negative or not. When I stepped back and looked at this, I saw the positive aspects of this mess: I rented an apartment for "less than it is worth," supposedly.   And, I really did have a have a beautiful Church view every day.

So, now what?   Well, first, I vowed to be more careful about remembering my digs, for heaven's sake.   And, I wrote a scathing letter of complaint to Owner's Direct.

As of this date, nearly a year later, I have yet to hear from Owner's Direct.   Will I rent from Owner's Direct again?   Maybe, but if I do it won't be from a company that coordinates more than one apartment.

On that, I will not capitulate.

CHAPTER THIRTEEN

Putting It All Together

Introduction
Pre-Planning Checklist
    At least six weeks before departure
    At least three weeks before departure
Essential Items Checklist

Introduction

All right! I have chapters and chapters of information, categorized in order of logical importance. All this information can be overwhelming. To overcome the magnitude of planning, I have created two checklists for international travel that are useful for everyone. That would be, dreamers who think they may travel someday, first-time travelers, as well as those who frequently travel.

Pre-Planning Checklist

This checklist brings together all the niggling details you need to understand and act on to get yourself ready to travel. Even if you haven't decided when or where you want you want to go, this check list makes for good planning.

At least Six Weeks before Departure:

_____See your doctor and get clearance to travel, if appropriate.

_____Update **prescriptions** and ensure you have more than enough medication for your trip.

132

_____Purchase a **medical bracelet or necklace**, if appropriate.

_____Make sure your **passport** is up to date: Your passport has to be valid for your entire trip. Not just the day you buy your tickets, or the day you leave. You can get or renew your passport through the mail or in person, and it typically takes four to six weeks. And while you can get the process expedited for an additional fee, it's best to not push your luck. (See Chapter Four.)

_____Check to see if your destination countries require **immunizations**. You can access that information on the U.S. Department of State website, as well. (See Chapter Twelve.)

_____Learn what's required for **visas**. Many countries don't require visas for U.S. passport holders. Others don't require an application, but collect a visa fee at the airport, not included in the price of your airfare. It can be complicated, but the U.S. State Department has a simple search tool to learn about visas, as well as vaccinations and other requirements. (See Chapter Four.)

At Least Three Weeks before Departure:

_____Register with the United States Department of State **STEP** online, not only for up-to-date security information but, also to alert them where you will be and for how long. (See Chapter Eight.)

_____Check on your **mobile phone plan**. As explained in CHAPTER SIX, look at what your current plan offers for international coverage, see if you need to change it to meet your needs, etc.

_____Check with your current **health insurance policy** regarding coverage abroad. Buy additional coverage is necessary, as discussed in Chapter Three.

_____Check your **credit cards.** Make sure you have credit cards <u>without</u> international transaction fees. If not, apply for a fee-free card. I discuss point-earing frequent flyer credits cards in Chapter Five. It's worth exploring.

_____Call your **bank and credit card companies** and call or visit your bank. Let them know your travel dates and destinations, otherwise, you may find these companies will deny access to your bank and block use of your cards. If you plan a long time away, be sure you are registered for online bill pay.

_____Consider acquiring a **debit card** without fees for cash advances when using an ATM.

_____Consider purchasing a **VPN.** If you get one, learn how to use it. It is essential if you plan to access your bank or credit card companies online. (See Chapter Seven.)

_____Using your cell phone, take a **photos** of all your important papers, including passport, driver's license, medical insurance, prescriptions, etc. for your phone app. Email them to yourself and save to iCloud or Dropbox. (See Chapter Eight.)

_____Check the **Apps** I list in Chapter Seven. I encourage you to load the "essential apps." Register and learn to use them.

_____Use TripIt or a similar app to maintain your transportation and lodging information.

_____Stop **snail mail** for the duration of your trip.

Essential Items Checklist

Besides on all of the typical items in your suitcase or back pack, such as tissues for the restrooms, wipes for all sorts of purposes, toiletries kits, band aids, laxatives, antacid medication, etc., I have listed below additional items that I always have with me.

I encourage you to take time to pack these items to be ready for most anything and also to save precious time searching for these items in unfamiliar places. Besides a camera which can be heavy, these items are small and lightweight. Furthermore, pack this stuff

_____**Athletic tape** is great to hold Band-Aids securely in place, especially on moist feet and toes. It's easy on the skin.

_____**Black electrical tape** comes in very handy. I use it to repair cables, secure a plug to my electrical outlet converter, and anything that needs to be repaired. I even used it once, in a pinch, to hold my broken sandals together.

_____**Cable** to charge your electronics is completely necessary. I have two. And, be sure to get a long cable, 6 feet or longer, especially because, unlike in the U.S., many hotels and apartments abroad have few outlets, often just on one wall, under the bed, or behind furniture…anywhere just beyond reach, it seems!

_____**Camera and peripherals** are necessities for traveling, obviously. I have a lightweight DCLR camera and I also carry an extra memory card, a battery, microfiber dust cloth, and a small tri-pod.

_____**Earplugs** are great, especially if you are a light sleeper; but, also if you find yourself next to a busy street or a loud nightclub.

_____**Ibuprofen** is nonsteroidal anti-inflammatory drug that is used for treating pain, fever, and inflammation. I find it useful for sore or tired muscles.

If you take aspirin, for your heart, for example, please educate yourself about the timing and interaction when taking both ibuprofen and aspirin.

_____**Instant coffee, tea, and sweetener** are great when you find yourself in an apartment with no time to shop for groceries and you need that morning coffee! Plus, coffee can be a great pick-me-up anywhere, anytime.

_____**Plastic spoons and forks** are especially useful when buying salads and non-finger foods from grocery stores while on the run.

_____**Sea Bands** are useful for motion sickness, nausea, morning sickness, cramps, stress reduction, and helping you get that sleep you desperately need.

_____**Zippered plastic bags** in various sizes have lots of uses: the largest sizes to pack panties, shorts, bras, sweaters, etc. (After placing items in the bag, I zipper it nearly shut, then roll the bag to remove air, hold, and zipper shut, to save space in my suitcase.); to store small plastic bottles of liquids, such as shampoo, as a special effort to protect from leakage; to keep healthy snacks; to hold wet swimsuits; and more.

CHAPTER FOURTEEN

Final Thoughts

Travel has changed my life. I lovingly blow in the wind and land in all sorts of destinations. Although, I have been volunteering and teaching English as a Second Language at the American University in Kosovo for months, it is unusual that I stay in one place over a month at a time.

This has been my life since January, 2015. And, all the while, I have been gathering information about how to make travel easier. Well, actually, it's more than that. There have been times I ran into seemingly insurmountable complications and barriers.

Like the time Turkish Airlines in Istanbul refused to give me a boarding pass for my flight to Madrid. And, when I found my debit card I use to get cash from the ATM and my credit card had both expired on the same day exactly when I was out of funds. Oh yeah, the time I couldn't see because of a dark shadow over my left eye. My retina had torn and I needed emergency surgery to avoid blindness.

Never the less, not once have I felt like I was in over my head or out of control. Not once did I think I needed to go back to the United States for a respite or to escape the unknown.

The sights and scenes I have experienced are too numerous to list here. Even if I tried, my words could never capture the overwhelming emotions I have felt throughout my journey.

My life is incredible, but, certainly not everyone's cup of tea. Perhaps this book will help you to maneuver travel trials and overcome any reluctance you may have to traveling internationally. Then, you too, could know an extraordinary life of travel.

APPENDICES

Appendix A: Definitions   140

Appendix B: Sources and Resources   142

Appendix C: Websites: Explore Potential Destinations   143

Appendix D: Disclaimer   144

APPENDIX A

Definitions

AI-powered bot: A computer program which conducts a conversation via auditory or textual methods used by Hipmunk and other websites. These programs are often designed to convincingly simulate how a human would behave as a conversational partner. Also called, Chatbots, this technology is typically used in dialog systems for various practical purposes including customer service or information acquisition. Some use sophisticated natural language processing systems, but many simpler systems scan for keywords within the input, then pull a reply with the most matching keywords, or the most similar wording pattern, from a database.

App - An app is computer software, or a program, most commonly a small, specific one used for mobile devices. The term app originally referred to any mobile or desktop application, but as more app stores have emerged to sell mobile apps to smartphone and tablet users, the term has evolved to refer to small programs that can be downloaded and installed all at once. You can find any app, for a smart phone, an android phone, and/or tablets online by googling "app" along with the service you want that app to perform, such as, foreign language app, travel app, exercise app, weight loss app, etc.

There are thousands of apps designed to run on today's phones and tablets. Some apps can be downloaded for free, while others must be purchased from an app store.

Brexit A term for the potential or hypothetical departure of the United Kingdom from the European Union.

Chatbots – Also known as AI-powered bot. (See above.)

Error fares - A reduced ticket price for a flight which comes as a result of a human or computer mistake.)

Kilogram (kg) - The kilogram is defined as being equal to the mass of the International Prototype of the Kilogram (IPK), a block of platinum-iridium alloy manufactured in 1889 and stored at the International Bureau of Weights and Measures in Sèvres, France.

Cool, eh? But, what we want to know is that one kilogram equals 2.20462 pounds.

Open jaw - A term denoting or relating to a trip in which an airline passenger flies in to one destination and returns from another. For example, an open jaw ticket might be departing from Madrid, to Paris, then to Lisbon, and back to Madrid.

Promo code or **promotional code** - A series of letters or numbers that allow you to get a discount on something.

VPN – Virtual Private Network - A virtual private network (VPN) is a technology that creates a safe and encrypted connection over a less secure network, such as the internet. VPN technology was developed as a way to allow remote users and branch offices to securely access corporate applications and other resources. A VPN is a method used to add security and privacy to private and public networks, like WIFI hotspots and the internet. It also allows you to "geo-spoof" your location in order to access services unfairly denied to you based on your geographical location.

APPENDIX B

Sources and Resources

Sources

Page 45: REAL ID,
www.state.gov/r/pa/prs/ps/2017/08/273747.htm

Page 101: Carry-on Luggage: Size and Weight Restrictions for International Flights according to SkyScanner:
https://www.skyscanner.com.au/news/airlines/carry-on-luggage-size-and-weight-restrictions-for-international-flights/

Resources

Please, access the following websites for more information about:

Passports:
www.travel.state.gov/content/passports/en/passports/FAQs.html

Pets and International Travel:
www.state.gov/m/fsi/tc/c10442.htm

TSA guidelines: www.tsa.gov

U.S. Embassies, Consulates, and Diplomatic Missions:
www.usembassy.gov

Wikipedia's List of Hub Cities
https://en.wikipedia.org/wiki/List_of_hub_airports

APPENDIX C

My favorite websites to explore destinations

Adventure Travel	www.adventure.travel
ACanela Expeditions	www.acanela.com
AirTravelWatchDog	www.airfarewatchdog.com
Condé Nast Traveler	www.cntraveler.com
Fathom	www.fathomaway.com
Fodor's Travel	www.fodors.com
G Adventures	www.gadventures.com
Jetsetter Magazine	www.jetsetter.com
The Lonely Planet	www.lonelyplanet.com
NomadicMatt	www.nomadicmatt.com
Oyster Magazine	www.oyster.com
Solo Travel	www.solotravelerworld.com
TourRadar	www.tourradar.com

APPENDIX D

Disclaimer

This book is presented solely for educational and entertainment purposes. The author and publisher are not offering it as legal, accounting, or other professional services advice. While best efforts have been used in preparing this book, the author and publisher make no representations or warranties of any kind and assume no liabilities of any kind with respect to the accuracy or completeness of the contents and specifically disclaim any implied warranties of merchantability or fitness of use for a particular purpose. Neither the author nor the publisher shall be held liable or responsible to any person or entity with respect to any loss or incidental or consequential damages caused, or alleged to have been caused, directly or indirectly, by the information or programs contained herein.

The information provided in this book is designed to provide helpful information on the subjects discussed. This book is not meant to be used, nor should it be used, to diagnose or treat any medical condition. For diagnosis or treatment of any medical problem, consult your own physician. The publisher and author are not responsible for any specific health or allergy needs that may require medical supervision and are not liable for any damages or negative consequences from any treatment, action, application or preparation, to any person reading or following the information in this book.

References are provided for informational purposes only and do not constitute endorsement of any websites or other sources. Readers should be aware that the websites listed in this book may change.

INDEX

A

accommodation (s), 29, **33**, 55, 69, 102

activity, 93, 111

Adriatic Sea, 112

adventure (s), iii, v, 14, 34, 41, 56, 82, 97, 99, 108, 111, 112, 113, 134, 156

Africa, 14, 134

agencies, 18, 30, 40, 58

aggregator, 30

AI, 17, 153

Airbnb, 17, 29, 46, 47, 64, 88, 96, 99, 106, 140

AirFareWatchDog, 16

airline (s), 15, 16, 18, 19, 30, 68, 69, 75,115, 116, 117, 118, 119, 154, 155

airport, 34, 37, 83, 85, 87, 97, 146

Airteck, xiii, 16, 126, 129, 130

alarm, 81

alcohol, 43, 104

Allianz, 48, 53, 54, 83, 139

Allianz Global Assist, 83

Allianz Global Assistance, 139

Allianz Travel Insurance, 48, 54

Allies, 78

alone, viii, 32, 55, 99, 103, 104, 109, 117

al-Qa'ida, 94

Amelia Island, 44

American Express, 16, 69, 70

Andes, v

animal, 42

apartment (s), 26, 29, 46, 47, 64, 99, 102, 103, 106, 121, 140, 141, 142, 143, 144, 148

app, 17, 75, 80, 81, 82, 83, 84, 86, 87, 88, 96, 97, 99, 102, 113, 114, 135, 147, 153

Appendix, 17, 152, 153, 155, 156, 157

Apple, 74, 100

apps, xi, 22, 45, 71, 72, 73, 75, 80, 81, 86, 88, 97, 98, 108, 110, 112, 113, 114, 134, 135, 147, 153

Apuan Alps, 77

architecture, 77, 89, 98, 106, 107, 112, 123

Asia, 17, 29, 85, 116, 127

aspirin, 148

assault, 94

Athletic tape, 147

Atlantic Ocean, 23, 44

ATM, 68, 147, 150

Australia, 22, 115, 116, 127, 129

Austria, vi, 60, 61, 106

authentic, vi, 39

automobiles, 20

B

Babbel, 88

backpack, 26, 75, 104, 109, 120, 121

baggage, 15, 49, 117, 118, 120, 138

balance, 68, 69, 86, 112

Bali, 129

Bangkok, 129

bank, 46, 67, 68, 81, 85, 86, 147

Bank of America, 67

banking, 84, 86

Barga, xi, 77, 78, 79

bargains, 127

Baron, 85, 86

Baroque, 107

bath, 31, 32

Battery Pack, xi, 71, 75

beach destinations, 128

bells and whistles, 15, 17

benefits, 18, 29, 34, 39, 44,

54, 55, 68, 70, 97, 112, 138

be-safe, 42

Bilbao, 23, 24

Black electrical tape, 148

BlueCross BlueShield of Rhode Island, 136

boat, 21

Bogota, 99, 100

booking, 14, 16, 17, 18, 19, 28, 29, 30, 33, 34, 85, 126, 140

Booking Sites, xiii, 15

booking websites, x,xiii, 14, 16, 18, 28, 29, 126

Booking.com, x, 30, 46, 88

borders, 59, 60, 62

Brexit, 61, 66, 153

British, 17, 23, 76, 77, 85, 115, 116

broad-gauge lines, 24

budget, 30, 31, 32, 33, 69, 73

bus, xii, 20, 21, 35, 71, 79, 102, 107, 126, 130, 131

C

Cable, 148

café, 37

caffeine, 123

Cambodia, 129

camera, 49, 56, 74, 90, 97, 116, 121, 124, 147, 148

Can I Eat This? App, 81

cancellation (s), 20, **49, 55, 56,**
  138

car rental insurance
  auto insurance, 139

Caribbean, **128**

carrier, **49, 55, 71, 72, 73, 74,**
  117, 130

castle, **39, 77, 78**

Centers for Disease Control
  and Prevention **CDC, 81, 83,**
  135

Central America, **134**

challenges, iii, **25, 137**

Chatbots, 153

check list, ix, **145**

checked, **47, 53, 109, 116,**
  117, 118, 119, 120

Chianti, **78**

Chile, v

China Airlines, **115, 116**

Cinque Terra, **79**

citizens, **57, 61, 62, 93, 94, 95**

Clock, 81

clothes, **118, 119, 133**

Cloud, **96, 97**

coat in a bag, **119, 120**

coconut oil, **111**

coffee
  tea, **37, 73, 123, 143, 148**

Communicate, xi, **71, 74**

Communication, xi, **71, 86**

company, **17, 29, 30, 34, 37,**
  49, 50, 53, 54, 55, 83, 96,
  137, 138, 139, 143, 144

computer (s), **17, 18, 35, 41,**
  46, 49, 56, 75, 83, 84, 86,
  88, 116, 121, 153

Conde Nast Traveler, **14**

Confession, **115, 121**

connection, **26, 46, 81, 83,**
  84, 97, 154

consulate (s), **93, 95, 137, 155**

consultant, **16**

Couchsurfing, x, **28, 29, 45**

country (ies), viii, **19, 21, 24,**
  26, 39, 43, 49, 55, 57, 59,
  60, 62, 71, 73, 74, 81, 82,
  83, 85, 92, 93, 94, 95, 107,
  110, 121, 130, 131, 132,
  134, 135, 137, 138

Craig's List, **118**

credit card (s), 50, 51, 52,
  53, 55, 67, 68, 69, 70, 84,
  85, 86, 87, 112, 147, 103,
  150

credit cards, 50, 51, 67, 68,
  69, 70, 84, 146

Croatia, **20, 60, 61**

cultures, **112**

Currency exchange, 81

Cusco, vi, xi, **32, 84, 89, 90**

customs, 86

Czech, 60, 61, 106, 107

D

DailyBurn, 113

data, 20, 72, 73, 74, 81, 83, 84, 87, 95, 97, 98

Death Coast Costa da Morta, vi

debit card, 16, 68, 96, 147

Department of Homeland Security, 59

departure, 21, 36, 43, 51, 61, 82, 97, 99, 145, 146, 153

Desna, 106, 107

destination(s), 14, 17, 18, 20, 21, 22, 23, 33, 53, 59, 71, 73, 74, 75, 82, 83, 95, 104, 106, 113, 127, 128, 129, 130, 137, 146, 147, 154, 156

destinations, 17, 20, 21, 22, 33, 75, 127, 128, 129, 147, 156

DiannAbroad, 29, 90

diet, 86, 113

discipline, 109

Disclaimer, xii, 152, 157

disease, v, 121, 136

doctor, 49, 96, 97, 108, 113, 136, 145

documents, xi, 83, 95, 96, 97, 102, 137

dogs, 39, 42, 43

dollars, 17, 85

drink, 24, 81, 101, 104, 110, 112, 113

Driver Safety Abroad, xii, 134, 137

Dropbox, 96, 97, 147

Dubrovnik, 112

Duolingo App, 88

dysfunction, 122

E

Earplugs earbuds, 148

EBay, 118

eDreams.com, 88

Egyptian, 107

embassy, 59, 93, 95, 137

emergency, x, 41, 48, 49, 51, 55, 83, 92, 93, 95, 97, 137

Emergency Medical Reunion EMR, x, 48, 54

Emirates, 115, 116

encrypted, 84, 87, 154

England, 43, 66

English, 25, 26, 76, 89, 100, 102, 106

error fare, 18, 153

escape, 43, 103, 130, 132,

142, 150

Etiquette, 28, 31, 35

Europe, v, 19, 21, 22, 24, 39,
44, 62, 66, 121, 127, 141

European, 19, 57, 59, 60, 61,
153

European Union, 57, 59, 60,
61, 153

Expedia.com, 30

Extremists, 94

F

Facebook Messaging
facebook, 74

FaceTime, 74

Fado, 112

feature (s), 16, 17, 51, 69, 70,
73, 81, 83, 97, 114

Federal Bureau of
Investigation, v

fee (s), viii, 15, 29, 35, 40, 49,
50, 51, 52, 62, 67, 68, 69,
72, 81, 89, 120, 121, 127,
136, 138, 141, 142, 143,
146, 147

ferries, x, xiii, 14, 20, 21, 131

festivals, 79, 103

Feve, x, 23, 24, 25, 26, 27, 130

finances, viii, 67, 68

FindMyiPhone App, 82, 99

FindMyPhone App, 82

first aid, 83, 109

Florence, 46, 78

Florida, 44, 87, 99, 128

Flynous, xiii, 18, 19, 126

foreign, 59, 68, 136, 137, 153

free, v, 15, 29, 33, 34, 39, 45,
50, 58, 59, 68, 71, 72, 74,
76, 78, 79, 80, 82, 84, 86,
87, 88, 93, 95, 97, 99, 101,
108, 112, 114, 146, 153

French, vi, ix, 24, 64, 100, 123,
124

frequent flyer, 15, 51, 52, 69,
70, 146

Frommer's, 30

frugal, 84, 85

G

Galacian, 23

Gandia, 20, 26, 123

geographical, 154

geo-spoof, 154

Germania, 120

Germans, 78

Google Drive, 96

Google Flights, xiii, 17, 18

GoogleMaps, 82

Gothic, 78, 107

government, 93, 94, 137

GPS, 71, 75, 82, 83, 98, 102,
141

Grand Atlas, vi
Greece, 20, 44, 60, 61
Guide, i, viii, ix, x, 36, 68
guidelines, xi, 28, 33, 38, 41,
    92, 101, 108, 117, 118,
    121, 155
Guido Bigarelli da Como, 78
guitar, vi, 26, 38, 106, 120,
    121

H

Hamilton, Ohio, 46
hand sanitizer, 110
health care, 49, 135
health insurance, 48, 96, 136,
    146
health issues, 135
health, 83, 109, 110, 135, 149
heart, 31, 38, 49, 64, 108, 110,
    112, 125, 148
HERE, 75, 82, 102
high season, 46, 127, 128, 140
hike, 110, 113
Hipmunk, xiii, 17, 153
home exchange, 44
Home Link, 44
Homeaway, 30
HomeExchange, 44
homeowners, 41, 42
Homestay, 30
hospital, 55, 83

hostel (s), x, 28, 29, 30, 31,
    32, 33, 34, 35, 36, 37, 38,
    46, 102
Hostel Bookers, 33
Hostel Celica, 36
hostelers, 31
**Hostelling International
    (HI)**, 34
hotel ()s), 17, 19, 22, 23, 29,
    30, 31, 32, 46, 47, 51, 76,
    81, 84, 94, 96, 98, 102,
    103, 121, 123, 125,
    129,148
hotspots, 154
House and Pet Sitting, 39
House Sitting, 40
House Sitting World, 40
House Swapping, x, 28, 38, 43
HouseCarers, 40
HouseSitMatch, 40
Housesitting, 28
Hub, xii, 126, 130, 155
Hub Cities, 130
HULU, 76, 85
hurricane
    hurricane belt, 128

I

Ibuprofen, 148
iCarHireInsurance, 139
identification, 58, 96, 103

identify theft, 85

immigration, 57, 86

Immunization (s), , 96

immunization (s), 83, 96,
135, 136, 146

Independent hostels, 33

India, 14, 129

Indonesia, 116, 129

information, viii, ix, 16, 17,
21, 22, 25, 32, 34, 40, 41,
45, 49, 50, 57, 58, 59, 60,
67, 69, 70, 72, 74, 75, 80,
81, 83, 85, 86, 87, 92, 93,
94, 95, 96, 97, 109, 118,
132, 134, 135, 137, 145,
146, 147, 153, 155, 157

inner voice, 45, 104

Instant Google Street View,
34

Insure My Trip, 48, 54

international, 16, 34, 53, 58,
71, 72, 73, 74, 81, 83, 96,
117, 145, 146, 155

International Drivers' License,
42

International Driving Permits,
137

internet, 23, 46, 74, 75, 84,
88, 96, 102, 111, 154

Intervac, 44

introspection, 112

iPad, 74

iPhone, 74, 82, 99

ISIS, 94

Istanbul, v, 128, 150

J

Japanese Encephalitis, 136,
137

jeans, 119

jewelry, 104, 120

journey, 23, 26, 27, 47, 102,
106, 107, 114

Jumbo Stay,

K

Kilogram (kg), 153

kilograms, 119

Kosovo, vi, xiii, 150

Kotor, Albania, 33

Krakow, xii, 140

Kuala Lumpur, 129

L

La Rosita Hostel, 31

Lake Erie, 43

language, 26, 82, 88, 101,
102, 153

Laos, 129

laptop (s), 71, 76, 88, 115,
116, 121

laundry, 32

leggings, 119

León, 23

lightweight, 119, 120, 147, 148

Lisbon, 75, 106, 112, 131, 154

listings, 29

Lo Coruna, 26

locals, 22, 24, 26, 39, 74, 77, 101, 124

location (s), 17, 21, 26, 34, 35, 44, 45, 49, 53, 55, 59, 76, 81, 82, 83, 85, 87, 102, 103, 104, 140, 141, 154

lock, 35, 41, 42, 82, 99, 104, 118

lodging, 16, 38, 29, 30, 33, 39, 45, 46, 47, 69, 80, 84, 127, 140, 147

logo, 16, 68

low season, 46, 127

Lucca,, 64, 77, 79

luggage, x, xi, 15, 48, 49, 51, 55, 97, 109, 111, 115, 117, 118, 140, 141, 155

M

Mac, 74

Madeira Island, Portugal, vi, 140

Madrid, 20, 150, 154

Malaysia, 116, 129

MapMyRun, 86, 113

Marinids, 131

Mark Smith, 21

Marrakesh, 131

Marseilles, France, 96

MasterCard, 16, 68

Matilda, 77, 78

medical bracelet or necklace, 146

Medical Information, 96

Medicare, 50, 136

medication, 83, 145, 147

Medina, 131, 133

meditation, 110, 114

meds, 109

membership, 33, 34, 40, 85

meningococcal meningitis, 136

metamorphosis, vi

Michigan State University Travel Clinic, 136

miles, 23, 51, 52, 69, 77, 107, 129

Milly, 131, 132, 133

Mind My House, 40

mobile, 17, 71, 72, 73, 74, 75, 83, 87, 146, 153

MobilePass, 86

Momondo, xiii, 17, 18, 46, 88

monsoon, 129

Morocco, Fez, vi, xii, 131, 133

mountains, v, vi, 23, 26, 38, 74, 78, 112

MyFitnessPal, 86, 109, 113

N

narrow-gauge, 23, 24

Netflix, 69, 86

New York, 17, 18, 85

New Zealand, 32, 116, 127

Nike Training Club, 86, 113

Nomador, 40

North America, 127, 128

northern coast, 23

Norwegian Airlines, 17, 85

notebook, 71, 102

notepad, 71

notes, xiii, 15, 17, 41, 51, 54, 65, 102, 117

O

off-line, 82

Oliva, 123

online, 14, 17, 20, 29, 30, 57, 64, 67, 68, 72, 73, 75, 76, 82, 84, 85, 86, 99, 139, 146, 147, 153

Open jaw, 18, 154

Open Table, 87

opera, vi, 64, 77, 79, 125

Oskar Schindler, 142

Oviedo, 23, 24

Owner's Direct, 130, 140, 144

owners, 43

P

pack, 72, 75, 100, 101, 109, 115, 119, 120, 121, 134, 143, 147, 149

Pania della Croce, 77

Parent Organization, 33

Paris, vi, 24, 113, 121, 128, 154

passenger (s), 20, 23, 58, 87, 115, **154**

passport (s), x, 57, 58, 62, 85, 87, 96, 134, 146, 147, 155

Passport Health,, 136

Peru, vi, xi, 32, 84, 89

Pet Sitting, 40

Philippines, 129

phone, cell phone, 16, 35, 41, 45, 56, 71, 72, 73, 74, 75, 76, 80, 81, 82, 83, 84, 86, 87, 88, 90, 96, 97, 98, 99, 100, 101, 102, 106, 111, 121, 141, 146, 147, 153

photos, 14, 37, 42, 56, 77, 89, 147

Pisa, 78, 79

plane, 21, 117

Pocket Yoga, 86, 114

points, 69, 70, 100

police, 40, 83, 99, 102

Ponte Vecchio, 46

Port Everglades, 87

possessions, vi, 118

pounds, 26, 85, 111, 115, 117, 119, 121, 154

Prague, xi, 106, 140

Praha Hlavni Nadrazi, 106

pregnant, 135

prescriptions, 96, 109, 145, 147

Prishtina, xiii

prison, 36, 94

privacy, 31, 36, 45, 84, 154

Promo code, 154

provider, 53, 55, 72, 73, 135

proXPM, 86

Puccini, x, 64, 65, 77

Q

Quito, Ecuador, 31

R

Rabat, 131

rabies, 136, 137

Real ID, 57, 58, 59, 155

References, 157

refunds, 29

religions, 37

Renaissance, 107

Renfe, 19, 20, 24, 25, 26, 27, 88

rental, 30

repairs, 138

restriction, 115

reviews, 35, 87

Ristorante Capretz, 78

Roamright, 48, 53, 55

Romanesque, 77, 107

Rome2Rio, x, xiii, 21, 22, 35, 102, 130

RosettaStone, 88

round the world, 129

Ryanair, 120

S

Sacahauayman, 89

Safe, xi, 92, 95

Safety, xi, xii, 92, 98, 99, 134, 137

San Giovanni Basilique, 64

San Miguel de Allende, Mexico, 43

San Sebastián, xi, 24, 25, 26, 46, 123, 124, 125

Santander, 23, 24, 26

saving, viii, 19, 31

Schengen Area, x, 57, 59, 60, 61, 62, 139

Schwab, 68

Sea Bands, 148

Secret Flying, xiii, 18, 19, 126

secured, 84, 101

security, 45, 58, 59, 60, 62, 70, 84, 93, 95, 118, 146, 154

Serchio Valley, 77, 78

service (s), 23, 24, 25, 29, 32, 34, 45, 46, 54, 55, 59, 67, 68, 73, 74, 81, 83, 84, 85, 86, 87, 88, 93, 95, 102, 138, 139, 153, 154, 157ervices, 59, 73, 83, 84, 93, 136, 138, 154, 157

shoes, 42, 110, 120, 121

shot, 89, 125, 136

shoulder season, 128

SIM, 73

Singapore, 18, 116, 129

sitters, 40

SixPack App Pro, 114

Sky Scanner, xiii, 18, 155

Skype, 75, 86, 111

sleep, 81, 111, 112, 123, 148

Smart Traveler Enrollment Program, STEP, 95, 102

snail mail, 43, 147

social security number, 85

"soft" targets, 94

solo, viii, 31, 45, 48, 54, 123, 140

South America, 32, 100, 121, 127, 134

Southeast Asia, 129

southern hemisphere, 127, 128

Spain, vi, 19, 20, 23, 24, 26, 46, 60, 61, 100, 106, 123, 130

spirit , spirited, v, 108, 111

Squaremouth, 48, 53

Stayz, 30

STEP, xi, 92, 95, 102, 146

STF Hostel, 34, 37

stranger, vi, 45, 103

streaming, 76, 85

suitcase, vi, 26, 106, 115, 118, 119, 121, 141, 147, 149

sun, 111

Supplemental Plan, 50

Sworkit, 86, 114

syndrome, 122

T

taxi, *taxis*, 31, 35, 37, 82, 87, 89, 102, 103, 107, 110, 123, 140, 141

technology, 71, 75, 80, 153, 154

temperatures, 129

tennis, v, 113, 119, 120

Teppy, 74

terrorists, 60, 94, 103

Thailand, 14, 129

"The Holiday," 43

The Lonely Planet, 14

The Man in Seat Sixty-One,
xiii, 21

The Mountain Hostel, 38

thieves, 92, 98, 99

tickets, 16, 17, 19, 20, 22, 26,
51, 55, 68, 71, 77, 117, 146

time zones, 76, 81

T-Mobile, 74

tolerance, 28

TorGuard, 86

TorVPN, 86

tour, 23

tourism, 94, 137

tourist (s), 23, 24, 98, 103,
107, 129

Tourist Offices, 25

train (s), 14, 17, 19, 20, 21,
22, 23, 24, 25, 26, 34, 35,
74, 77, 79, 85, 102, 106,
123, 130

transformational, vii

transformative, vii

transportation, x, xiii, 14,
16, 20, 21, 22, 32, 35,
49, 55, 80, 94, 102, 127,
130, 147

translate, 83

Translator App, 87

Transportation, x, xiii, 14, 22

travel, iii, v, vi, vii, viii, ix, 14,
16, 17, 18, 19, 21, 22, 23,
28, 30, 39, 48, 49, 50, 51,
52, 53, 54, 55, 58, 59, 61,
62, 66, 68, 69, 71, 72, 80,
83, 86, 92, 93, 94, 95, 96,
97, 102, 106, 107, 108,
111, 112, 114, 117, 118,
126, 128, 129, 130, 132,
134, 135,136, 139, 145,
147, 150, 151, 153, 155,
156, 170

Travel Alerts, 92

Travel assistance, 138

Travel medical insurance,
49

Travel Medicine ISTM, 135

traveler, viii, 30, 38, 45, 54,
84, 85, 108, 138, 140

Traveler Profile, 97

Traveling, 108, 110, 112

Travelocity, 18, 30

TravelSmart, 83

TravWell App, 83

trip, v, 14, 18, 23, 26, 44, 49,
50, 52, 53, 54, 55, 56, 70,
73, 74, 75, 81, 83, 86, 87,
93, 97, 109, 110, 126, 127,
129, 134, 135, 137, 138,

145, 146, 147, 154

Trip Insurance, x, 48, 49

Trip Planner, 16, 130

Tripit, 83, 84, 96, 97, 147

Trivago, 30

TrustedHousesitters, 41

TSA, 117, 118, 155

Turkey, v, vi

Turkish Airlines, 150

typhoid, 136

U

U.S. Customs and Border
   Patrol (CBP), 87

U.S. Department of State, xi,
   57, 59, 62, 95, 102, 146

U.S. Embassy (ies), 93, 95,
   137, 155

Uber, 22, 75, 87, 102, 103

UK, United Kinigdom, 17, 85,
   139

United States U.S., viii, 19, 49,
   53, 57, 69, 72, 76, 85, 86,
   92, 93, 95, 117, 136, 137,
   146

Universe v

V

vacation, 17, 23, 29, 30, 44,
   73, 126

vaccination (s), 135, 136, 146

vaccines, 134, 135, 136

Vamonos, 90

VBRO, 30

vehicles, 94, 138

Venice, 128

Viber, 75, 86, 111

Video, 74, 75

Vienna, 106, 140

Vietnam, 129

Vignette, x, xi, xii, 23, 46, 64,
   77, 89, 106, 123, 130, 131,
   140

Virtual Travel Assistant, 17

Visa (s), x, 16, 57, 59, 61, 62,
   68, 69, 96, 146

Visual Timeline Graphs, 17

vital, 85, 86

vitamins, 109

VPN, 17, 46, 76, 84, 85, 86,
   147, 154

Virtual Private Network,
   154

W

walk, 110

weather, 20, 56, 76, 119, 127,
   128, 129

Weather channel, 87

website (s), 14, 15, 17, 19, 20,
   21, 22, 25, 29, 30, 38, 44,
   45, 46, 59, 61, 62, 70, 72,

73, 88, 90, 95, 115, 135,
140, 143, 146, 153, 155,
156, 157

weight, 115, 116, 117, 119,
121, 153, 155

Western Europe, 19

WhatsApp, 75, 86, 111

WIFI, x, 46, 47, 71, 73, 74,
81, 84, 87, 113, 140, 154

wine, 109

wireless, 74, 87

WiTopia., 86

Wizz Air, 15

world, v, vi, 16, 20, 21, 30,
33, 34, 36, 37, 38, 39, 46,

50, 53, 59, 62, 68, 72, 76,
83, 92, 99, 106, 112, 122,
126, 129, 131, 132, 134,
139

World Nomads, 48, 54, 55

Worldwide Caution, xi, 92, 93,
95

write, 40, 44, 112

Y

yellow fever, 134, 136

Z

Zippered plastic bags, 149

zloty, 142

ABOUT THE AUTHOR

Following a career in higher education, Dr. Diann Schindler retired to Florida and dabbled in tennis, music, and writing. However, her lifelong dream of traveling the world consumed her and, eventually, she could no longer resist. In January of 2015, she sold her house, her car, and all her possessions, save her guitar, tennis racket and just enough clothing to begin her life of travel .

In June of 2017, Dr. Schindler published her first novel, "Just A Girl" – which Amazon ranked the sixth best coming-of-age fiction for 2017. At the time of publishing "The Essential Guide to a Life of Travel," she had traveled to over thirty countries and was embarking on a lengthy journey in Asia.

She plans to start writing her third book, in December, 2017, while on the Mediterranean Sea in Malta. She said, "This next novel will be about lust, love, deceit, intrigue…and anything else that emerges when my Muse lovingly takes hold of me!"

For more information, access her website: www.DiannAbroad.com. Subscribe to her newsletter. Check out her blog, photography, podcasts, and more. You can also find her on Facebook: DiannAuthor. Please write to her through her website or by email at diann@diannabroad.com.

She loves hearing from her readers!

Made in the USA
Columbia, SC
10 December 2017